THE FOUNTAINHEAD REFERENCE GUIDE

A to Z

EMRE GURGEN

authorHOUSE®

AuthorHouse™
1663 Liberty Drive
Bloomington, IN 47403
www.authorhouse.com
Phone: 1 (800) 839-8640

Published by AuthorHouse 10/10/2019

ISBN: 978-1-7283-3072-3 (sc)
ISBN: 978-1-7283-3073-0 (hc)
ISBN: 978-1-7283-3071-6 (e)

Library of Congress Control Number: 2019915934

Print information available on the last page.

INTRODUCTION

Since this *Reference Guide* organizes *most* of *The Fountainhead's* facts by major character, minor character, journalism, chronology, buildings, symbols, places, and more, it will help students link their theories about the book to the book's particulars. So pupils write precise papers about the novel's exact happenings not floating treaties that abstract away from the novel's concretes. Accordingly, this *Reference Guide* focuses on the book's who's, what's, when's, where's, and why's. So it can help all people, whether they are objectivists or not, connect their theories on the novel to the book's empirical evidence. To the book's exact data-points. So high-school students writing papers for their teachers, undergraduate bachelors writing essays for their instructors, graduate students writing theses for their professors, doctoral candidates writing dissertations for their mentors, and independent scholars writing books for the general public, can write accurate critiques about *The Fountainhead* from a precise point-of-view. So learners not only induce from the book's particulars the book's universals but also so they can understand the novel according to how Ayn Rand conceived it and how Objectivist Intellectuals critique it.

That said, this *Reference Guide* is not simply a *verbatim* organization of *The Fountainhead's* facts in Ayn Rand's own words. It also analyzes scenes from the book, symbols from the book, narrative techniques used in the book, as well as its' characters' thoughts, motives, actions, and emotions in my own words. Thus, even though 10 % of this *Reference Guide* is my own unique analysis – while 90 % of it is a neutral presentation of the novel's facts – scholars may still be refreshed by it not only because it offers comprehensive data about *The Fountainhead* organized in an easily understandable format but also because my analysis is not simply objectivist – or non-objectivist – boilerplate. It is my own *sui generis* views.

Additionally, people may also find this *Reference Guide* helpful since it tables Ayn Rand's fiction and non-fiction according to title, publisher, division, imprint, location, edition, and reprint. Ergo, pupils who wish to understand Ayn Rand's scope of ideological production can see her intellectual output illustrated in one place.

Moreover, students can also use this *Reference Guide* to direct themselves to the books, lectures, and articles of 58 Objectivist Intellectuals on topics such as teaching values in the classroom, study methods and motivations, the self-made scholar, and more. They can do this via an *Objectivist Intellectuals* spreadsheet placed at the back of this book that guides understudies to Andrew Bernstein's *Cliff Notes*, for instance, or Robert Mayhew's *Essays*, for example, as well as the essays, presentations, and books of other Objectivist Intellectuals, too, which together synopsize *The Fountainhead*; summarize its four parts; analyze its' 15 main characters; and offer essays on topics such as how the novel inspires a spirit of youth, how people are to understand the rape scene, how humor is used in the book, and more.

In sum, this *Reference Guide* is not only useful because it directs pupils to learn how Ayn Rand's philosophy can benefit them pedagogically but it is also useful because it guides pupils to understand how her philosophy applies to issues such as justice, free-will, happiness, and goodwill.

Finally, to promote a clearer picture of Ayn Rand's architectural universe, this *Reference Guide* defines 39 design terms in a back-matter glossary, so people can better understand how the *Fountainhead's* buildings reflect the esthetic philosophies of its' builders.

In brief, since this *Reference Guide* organizes *The Fountainhead's* facts more fully than any other source I know of – including any objectivist source – it makes a significant intellectual contribution to our understanding of Ayn Rand's second greatest novel.

EXPLANATION OF THIS BRIEF *FOUNTAINHEAD* *REFERENCE GUIDE* / APPEAL TO DR. PEIKOFF TO ALLOW ME TO PUBLISH THE FULL VERSION

Though, originally, I wrote a complete *Fountainhead Reference Guide* that delivered on my introduction's promises, sadly, I cannot share it with you, right now, because I cannot secure copyright permission, presently.

However, I can share with you a condensed version of my study primer, which elucidates *The Fountainhead* by doing seven things. First, it clarifies the novel by summarizing, in one sentence, the essence of the book's 152 characters. Second, it explains their beings in 91 analytical sections. Third, it visualizes the book's buildings by defining 39 architectural words. Fourth, it explains how I learned about Ayn Rand's philosophy, what I have done to support it, and why I should be trusted. Fifth, it tables Ayn Rand's fiction-and-non-fiction in a chart, so you understand her intellectual output. Sixth, it illustrates, in a spreadsheet, how objectivist intellectuals have applied Ayn Rand's philosophy to different fields of thought, so you understand how her viewpoints apply to modernity. Seventh, it enumerates works I have read, highlighted, and studied to understand *The Fountainhead*, so you comprehend the scholarship I will use to support my forthcoming *Fountainhead Analyzed Essay Book*.

Though, this information clarifies *The Fountainhead*, clarifies Ayn Rand's philosophy, clarifies Objectivism, and clarifies my next book, unfortunately, I cannot cast full-light on *The Fountainhead* currently, since Dr. Peikoff (the copyright owner) "does not review unsolicited manuscripts." Nor does he "engage in philosophical work anymore, [since] he is now fully retired." Ergo, I cannot send him my book, since he will neither look at nor evaluate it.

Clearly, Dr. Peikoff has a right to not view unsolicited manuscripts; for he is a busy man who lacks time to ponder his daily philosophic mail. I understand that. He also has the right to disengage from philosophy altogether, since, at age 85, he has *already* defended Objectivism ably, by explaining AR's philosophy for over 65 years. His sustained efforts, as a result, to support Objectivism, by writing books, delivering talks, and teaching classes, has won Dr. Peikoff the right to enjoy his life's twilight, doing whatever he likes. For, great men, like him, who have fought, and won, the good fight, by being brave, intelligent, and moral, deserve to enjoy their sunset years.

Even though Dr. Peikoff is right to focus on his own goals – not what I want of him – I think that my *Reference Guide* does align with his goals, by logically codifying a book he loves. Thus, enabling him to transmit his basic principles to people. Alternatively, if he thinks my *Reference Guide* is pretty good – but not perfect – he can ask someone to correct it, if he thinks Objectivism will benefit from its' polished publication. Lastly, if he thinks my book is hopelessly flawed, beyond repair, he can tell me that, in his own words, instead of not engaging. So I not only understand why my book is mistaken but I also realize how to fix it.

Incidentally, since Dr. Peikoff spent decades of his life studying, analyzing, writing and speaking about *The Fountainhead* he should value a *Reference Guide* that illuminates the novel so clearly. Because I believe his goal is to create an intellectual climate that is friendly to Ayn Rand, friendly to her philosophy, and friendly to her ideas. Ergo, I believe that my *Reference Guide* will generate this goodwill towards her, in certain circles – where she has not been liked until now – because its' author, me, is a neutral party. With no axe to grind. For I am not affiliated with – nor loyal to – any organization, institution, or thought movement, whatsoever. Which intellectual independence renders me a dispassionate, non-biased, truth-seeker, who is less likely to antagonize certain people, with extant associations.

Dr. Peikoff *should* also allow me to self-publish my entire *Reference Guide*, since it induces clarity in pupils' minds by enabling scholars to go over-and-over the novel's facts again-and-again, so that when they write their papers, they can easily recall facts from their memories, or look up facts they know exist, without pouring over the book, like I did, for 18 months.

Further, if someone wrote a *Reference Guide* that conveyed my values, I would not care who wrote it, why they wrote it, nor what people said about this person. Just the reverse. I would judge the book by its inherent worth only. Regardless of what others thought.

To elaborate, if Dr. Peikoff uses his own objective judgment (which he does) to judge for himself what to do (which he does) instead of yielding to the subjective opinions of others (which he does not) I am confident that he will either grant me instant permission to publish. To help clarify Ayn Rand's moral code. Or require me to refine my book, so he can allow later publication. Or deny me permission outright, with solid reasoning why.

Ergo, to help him decide, I'd like Dr. Peikoff to take a brief moment, from his retirement, to read some of my materials. Then, after he decides, return to loving his wife, loving his family, traveling the world, or whatever else he likes.

Alternatively, if Dr. Peikoff does not want to endorse my book publicly, he can let me publish it privately, by telling penguin to authorize publication, without using his name. Without staking his reputation. Without vouching for my book. But rather authorizing a *Reference Guide* – that mostly aligns with Objectivist virtues and values – without explicitly sanctioning it.

That said, casting daylight on my *Reference Guide* does not mean Dr. Peikoff approves of, condones, or sanctions my book completely. What it does mean is that he values my study guide – on some level – insofar as it enables pupils to concretize their understanding of *The Fountainhead*, succinctly, so they support their objectivist views ably – with facts, evidence, and logical inference.

In my view, Dr. Peikoff should allow me to support Objectivism by letting me somehow publish my book, so his acolytes, "who do still engage in philosophical work," comprehend the *Fountainhead* better.

In sum, since my *Fountainhead Reference Guide* may enable objectivism to shine more directly, sparkle more brightly, and illuminate everything more clearly, it should be published. So that it breathes new life into Objectivism, by casting factual sunlight on *The Fountainhead*.

Until it is fully published, though, this condensed *Fountainhead Reference Guide* is all I can offer. Sorry.

CALL TO OBJECTIVIST INTELLECTUALS FOR EDITING / EXPLANATION OF MY NEXT BOOK

Though I *hope* that eventually my full *Reference Guide* will be approved by the *Ayn Rand Institute* and endorsed by *Objectivist Intellectual(s)* in its current form it is unsanctioned by both. But it *may* be certified by these two sources later if they believe it transmits Objectivism to people accurately in essential terms. Thus, to merit their blessing I will modify [1] this *Reference Guide* by removing inaccurate analysis (if there is any); tweak the analysis that already exists (so it reads perfectly); and edit this book for grammar, syntax, and punctuation (if required).

In exchange for an *Objectivist Intellectual* editing this *Reference Guide* I will happily let this person put his or her name in the by-line of this book—perhaps first—if their contribution is significant enough. In my view, Andrew Bernstein is the best person for this job, since he is great at linking *The Fountainhead's* facts to an accurate explanation of those facts. But if he cannot revise this book because he has other projects he needs to focus on, maybe another professional objectivist who is less busy, finds my analysis accurate, and trusts me, can help me perfect this book. So it is worth being formally published by an appropriate publisher.

But if presently no Objectivist Intellectual can help me refine this book because they are unsure what will come of it, maybe they could write something about it in the future. When they see that my next book links *The Fountainhead's* facts to Ayn Rand's explanation of those facts to the ideas of proven Objectivist intellectuals to my own original Objectivist analysis. Perhaps then they could write a foreword, or an afterword, or a brief quote, since I will produce theses I hope they can agree with. For they certainly agree with Ayn Rand's ideas, their own ideas, and

---

[1] Surely Objectivist philosophers, who have been studying Objectivism for decades, understand when my ideas align with AR's thoughts and when they do not. That is why I want them to edit my book. So it 100 % aligns.

the books facts. Ergo, they will *probably* agree with my own Objective thoughts based on this data. And if there is any element in my next book they disagree with they can fix it too by co-authoring that book with me as well. For my follow-up *Fountainhead* book will link Ayn Rand's *Fountainhead* analysis (as expressed in her letters, journals, lectures, and non-fiction books) to the thinking of Objectivist Intellectuals (as expressed in their study guides, essays, and talks) to my own Objectivist ideas (as expressed in this *Reference Guide*, my diary, and notes).

If, after reading my next book, Objectivist Intellectuals think I have linked Ayn Rand's ideas, their ideas, and my ideas along Objectivist lines maybe then an appropriate individual can endorse both my books. Especially if this person sees that my next book expresses the values of America's founding spirit – capitalism, individualism, and reason – as shown by a non-objectivist intellectual named Douglas J. Den Uyl in his book *The Fountainhead: An American Novel*.

In brief, I invite Andrew Bernstein (or any Objectivist Intellectual) to co-author, or revise, or edit, or write something about this *Reference Guide* not only because I want to understand Ayn Rand's philosophy better—so I can accurately transmit it to youths—but also sharing a by-line with an Objectivist Intellectual will reward me for a difficult job well done.

HOW TO USE MY FULL *FOUNTAINHEAD* REFERENCE GUIDE

To use my full reference guide, which is on my academia.edu account, please look-up (alphabetically) the specific information you are searching for within the relevant section. The twelve sections are:

1. Major Characters (28)
2. Minor Characters (124)
3. Buildings (37)
4. Journalism (9)
5. Groups of People (20)
6. Chronology
7. Sundry Concepts (6)
8. Symbols (27)
9. Places (6)
10. Architectural Terms (39)
11. Ayn Rand's Fiction and Non-Fiction (23)
12. Objectivist Intellectuals (58)

MAJOR CHARACTERS (28)

1) **Alvah Scarret** (*The Banner's* Chief Editor. Voices Tawdry Populist Sentiments)
2) **Austen Heller** (*Chronicle* Journalist Who Supports Freedom Fighters Everywhere)
3) **Caleb Bradley** (Fraudster Who Organizes The Monadnock Valley Summer Resort)
4) **Catherine Halsey** (Idealist Who Toohey Tricks Into Betraying Her Soul)
5) **Claude Stengel** (Chief Draftsman & Head Designer of Francon & Hyer)
6) **Dean of Stanton** (Classical Academic Who Voices Traditional Values)
7) **Dominique Francon** (Highly Intelligent Temperamental Idealist Who Is The Only Woman Worthy of Roark)
8) **Ellsworth (Monkton) Toohey** (Soul-Stealer and Power-Monger Extraordinaire)
9) **Gail Wynand** (Evil Genius & Second-Hander Who Should Have Been a First Hander Like Roark)
10) **Gordon L. Prescott** (Nihilistic Architect)
11) **Augustus (Gus) Webb** (New Left Thug Who Will Be Toohey's Strong Man Once He Grabs Power)
12) **Guy Francon** (Classically Trained Phony Gentleman Architect)
13) **Henry Cameron** (Roark's Mentor & Father of the Modern Skyscraper)
14) **Hopton Stoddard** (Guilt-Ridden Religionist Who Wants To Repent By Building a Temple to The Human Spirit)
15) **Howard Roark** (Original Creator and Arch First Hander. He Represents Perfection)

16) **Joel Sutton** (Loves Everybody Indiscriminately And Therefore Values Noone According To Their Virtues)
17) **John Erick Snyte** (Mongrel Architect Who Weaves Discordant Building Styles Into Jumbled Monstrosities)
18) **Kent Lansing** (Persuades Aquitania's Board To Accept Roark's Designs)
19) **Constance (Kiki) Holcombe** (Superficial Social Hostess Who Sponsors Architectural Salons)
20) **Louisa Keating** (Meddling Mother Who Pushes Her Son Peter To Do What Is Best For Her Not What Is Best For Him)
21) **Lois Cook** (Second-Handed Hippy Artist a La Gertrude Stein)
22) **Lucius N. Heyer** (Feeble Blue-Blood Who Is Only a Partner at Francon & Heyer So Guy Francon Can Use His Name and Lineage To Bedazzle Other Withered Aristocrats)
23) **Mike Donnigan** (Able Builder Who Is Also a First-Hander Like Roark. He is the Best of Everyman)
24) **Peter Keating** (Second-Hander & Social Metaphysical Architect Who Just Wants People To Like Him)
25) **Ralston Holcombe** (Renaissance Architect & President of The Architectural Guild of America. He Designs State Capitols)
26) **Roger Enright** (Self-Made Multi-Millionaire Who First Commissions Roark To Build an Apartment Building. Then Buys Cortlandt For Roark to Rebuild)
27) **Steven Mallory** (Genius Sculptor With The Most Expressive Eyes Possible. Tries to Kill Toohey. Loves Roark because Roark Lets him Work His Way)
28) **Tim Davis** (Favored Draftsmen at Francon & Hyer Who Keating Supplants. Sadly, He Thinks Keating is His Best Friend But Keating is Really His Worst Enemy)

MINOR CHARACTERS (124)

1) **Allen's Daughter** (Stars in Ike's Plays)
2) **Andrew Colson** (Francon Uses Him as an Excuse to Leave Keating Alone with Dominique)
3) **Athelstan Beasley** (A.G.A. Columnist)
4) **Billings** (Snytes' Office Manager)
5) **Mr. Brooks** (Slum Lord)
6) **Cornelius (Neil) Dumont** (Partner at Keating & Dumont)
7) **Mr. & Mrs. Dale Ainsworth** (Socialites)
8) **Mrs. Dunlop** (Commissions Stengel)
9) **Dwight Carson** (Wynand Corrupts Him)
10) **The Eddington's** (Members of The Social Register)
11) **Eugene Pettingille** (Septuagenarian A.G.A. Member)
12) **Eve Layton** (Mitchell Layton's Wife)
13) **Falk's Brother** (Secretary to Lancelot Clokey)
14) **Mrs. Gillespie** (Kiki Holcombe's Party Goer)
15) **Mr. Grant & Mr. Hubbard** (Board Members of the Janss-Stuart Real Estate Company)
16) **Mr. & Mrs. Gilbert Colton** (Owners of Colton California Pottery)
17) **Grace Parker** (Catherine Halsey's Friend)
18) **Harding** (The *Banner's* Acting Managing Editor)
19) **Mr. Holt** (Thinks Keating is the Architect of the Century)
20) **Homer Slottern** (Department Store Owner)
21) **Mr. Huseby** (Cosmetic Mogul)
22) **Ike (The Genius)** (Failed Playwright Who Writes *No Skin Off Your Ass / Nose*)
23) **Mr. Inskip** (Dominique Dissuades Him From Hiring Roark)
24) **Jackie** (Subnormal Child)
25) **Jackson** (*Banner* Employee Who Quits During *Banner* Strike)

26) **Jessica Pratt** (Marries Her Sister Renee Pratt to Homer Slottern)
27) **Jimmy Kearns** (The *Banner's* Old Drama Critic)
28) **John Fargo** (Owns The Fargo Department Store)
29) **Jules Fougler** (The *Banner's* New Drama Critic)
30) **Mrs. Jones** (Hears Dominique's Compassion Speech)
31) **Mrs. Lonsdale** (Hires Keating)
32) **Lancelot Clokey** (The *Banner's* Foreign Correspondent)
33) **Loomis** (Henry Cameron's Draftsmen)
34) **Mitchell Layton** (The *Banner's* Main Stockholder)
35) **Mrs. Moreland** (Rich Woman With A Fancy House)
36) **Nathaniel Janss** (Owns The Janss-Stuart Real Estate
37) Company)
38) **Palmer** (Sculptor)
39) **Mrs. Palmer** (Slum Lord)
40) **The Palmers** (The Keating's Dine With Them to Get Commissions)
41) **Mr. Parker's Son** (Redraws Manhattan Bank Building)
42) **Pasquale Orsini** (Mason Roark Sends To Repair Dominique's Fireplace)
43) **Pat Mulligan** (Honest Police Captain)
44) **Professor Peterkin** (Stanton Professor of Design)
45) **The Policeman Who Tells Toohey to Scram**
46) **Rene Pratt-Slottern** (Kept Creature)
47) **President of Stanton** (Shakes Keating's Hand During Graduation / Dean Takes a Chance With His Temper When Thinking of Reinstating Roark)
48) **Roark's Secretary** (Announces Dominique / Tells Roark Mallory Shot Toohey / Makes an Appointment With Wynand / Admits Wynand)
49) **Robert L. Mundy** (Raised on a Plantation)
50) **Ronny Pickering** (Rich Alcoholic Donner to *The New Frontiers*)
51) **Rotten Beet Leaf Thrower** (Wynand Feels Responsible For Creating Her)
52) **Simpson** (Cameron's Receptionist / Draftsmen)

53) **Superintendent of Rock Quarry** (Talks to Dominique / Tells Roark Not to Stare / Tells Dominique That Many Quarry Workers Have Jail Records)

54) **Mrs. Symington** (Synte Builds a Leaky Residence For Her)

55) **Mr. Symons** (Commissions Keating [Not Roark] to Build a Skyscraper)

56) **Mr. Talbot** (Owns the *Courier*)

57) **Ted Shlinker** (Keating's Stanton Competitor)

58) **Valerian Bronson** (Sculptor)

59) **Vincent Knowlton** (Blue Blood Who Keating Flatters)

60) **Mrs. Wayne Wilmot** (Heller Worshipper)

61) **Mr. Weidler** (Board Member of the Manhattan Bank Building)

62) **The Young Man** (Needs Hope & Inspiration From Roark)

63) **Betsy** (Aquitania Hotel Board Member)

64) **Mr. Harper** (Aquitania Hotel Board Member)

65) **Mr. Macy** (Aquitania Hotel Board Member)

66) **Mr. Palmer** (Aquitania Hotel Board Member)

67) **Mrs. Pritchett** (Aquitania Hotel Board Member)

68) **Mr. Thompson** (Aquitania Hotel Board Member)

69) **Mr. Thorpe** (Aquitania Hotel Board Member)

70) **Unnamed Aquitania Board Member**

71) **Old Watchman** (Aquitania Hotel Security)

72) **Mr. Flemming** (Pencil King / Heller's Friend)

73) **Allen** (Head of the *Banner's* Copy Desk)

74) **Falk** (The *Banner's* Copy Reader)

75) **Manning** (A *Banner* Slotman)

76) **Sally Brent** (A *Banner* Columnist)

77) **Cortlandt's Director of Social Recreation**

78) **Cortlandt's Policeman**

79) **Cortlandt's Night Watchman**

80) **Dimple William's** (Actress Cosmo-Slotnick Pictures / Columnist / Ex-Lover of Steven Mallory / Lover of Mr. Cosmo)

81) **Pratt Purcell** (Actor who Acts as Pardoner in *Wives for Sale*)

82) **Sally O'Dawn** (Actress Who Auditions for *I'll take a Sailor*)

83) **Mr. Shupe** (President of Cosmo-Slotnick Pictures)

84) **Mrs. Shupe** (Wife of President of Cosmo-Slotnick Pictures)
85) **Caretaker** (Francon Colonial Mansion)
86) **Caretaker's Wife** (Francon Colonial Mansion)
87) **Dominique's Maid** (Announces Visitors / Gets Toohey Cointreau / Tells Roark Dominique Can't See Him)
88) **Dominique's Mother** (Queenly Aristocrat / Gracious and Severe / Chatelaine of a Countryside Village in Connecticut)
89) **Young Poet** (Woos Dominique)
90) **Bennett** (Prominent Draftsman at Francon & Heyer Who Later Works for Keating)
91) **Cooper** (Francon's Draftsman Whose Pictures of a DC Museum are Rejected by a Client)
92) **Williams** (Francon's Draftsman Whose Pictures of a DC Museum are Rejected by a Client)
93) **Chief of Engineering** (Francon & Heyer)
94) **Jim Ferris** (Liberal Businessman Who is the Principal Partner at Ferris & Symes)
95) **Billy Shultz** (Liberal Businessman Who Owns *Vimo Flakes*)
96) **Bud Harper** (Liberal Businessman Who Owns *Toddler Togs*)
97) **Chairman** (Manhattan Bank)
98) **Mr. Whitford Sanborn** (Industrialist Who Hires Roark Because He Loves an Office Building Cameron Designed for Him)
99) **Mrs. Whitford (Fanny) Sanborn** (Tries to Dictate to Roark How To Build Her House)
100) **Richard Sanborn** (Brilliant Forlorn Former College Student Who Loves Roark's House So Much He is The Only Person to Live in It)
101) **June Sanborn** (Fatuously Smitten With Roark)
102) **Aunt Rosalie** (Mrs. Sanborn's Elderly Aunt Who May Have Difficulty Climbing Roark's Circular Stairs)
103) **Mrs. Applebee** (Mrs. Sanborn's Friend Who Thinks Roark's House Looks Like a Shoefactory)

104) **Miss Davitt** (Mrs. Sanborn's Friend Who Changes Her Opinion of Roark From Artistic to Phony Once She Learns Roark is Not Famous)

105) **Mrs. Hooper** (Mrs. Sanborn's Friend Who Calls Roark's House *Crude*)

106) **Mr. Hulburt** (Mrs. Sanborn's Friend Who Thinks Roark's Ceilings Will Collapse)

107) **Mr. Melander** (Mrs. Sanborn's Friend Who Says He Would Not Have Roark's House as a Present)

108) **Mrs. Walling** (Mrs. Sanborn's Friend Who Calls Roark's House Preposterous)

109) **Senator Eldridge** (Wynand's Washington Senator)

110) **Senator Hazelton** (Senator Lampooned as a Gallant Gallstone)

111) **Judge** (Stoddard Trial)

112) **Stoddard's Attorney**

113) **Aunt Adeline** (Toohey's Aunt. She Hates Ellsworth)

114) **Mary Toohey** (Toohey's Mother. She Dotes on Ellsworth)

115) **Horace Toohey** (Toohey's Father / Shoestore Manager / Dislikes Ellsworth)

116) **Helen Toohey** (Toohey's Older Sister / Catherine Halsey's Mother / Neglected by Mary Toohey / Aunt Adeline's Favorite)

117) **Drippy Munn** (Toohey's Snot-Nosed Classmate Who Is the Son of a Widowed Seamstress)

118) **Willie Lovett** (Toohey's Classmate Whose Father Own's a Dry-Goods Store)

119) **Skinny Dix** (Toohey's Emaciated Classmate Who Suffers From Infantile Paralysis)

120) **Thomas L. Foster** (Noted Philanthropist Who Bequeaths Money to Toohey)

121) **Rusty Hazelton** (Toohey's Less Than Studious Classmate)

122) **Pat Noonan** (Toohey's Capable Childhood Schoolmate)

123) **Billy Wilson** (Toohey's Schoolmate Who Toohey Consoles)

124) **Toohey's Valet** (Serves Keating & Toohey Tea)

ANALYTICAL SECTIONS

ANALYSIS (91)

(1) ANALYSIS OF WHY CATHERINE DOES NOT CONTACT PETER:

Because Catherine views selflessness as a virtue she does not believe in pleasing herself. Rather she denies herself by failing to develop a romance with Peter. Thus, she practices extreme self-denial, since she feels she must not make selfish demands on Peter's time. Ergo, she never calls, writes, meets, or wires Keating. Instead she relishes the rare occasions when he comes to her. Never knowing when he will show-up next, be it the next day the next week or months later, Catherine feels she must wait for Peter to initiate and sustain contact. Thus, she waits for him to make the next move. For him to call, wire, or reach out to her in some way. Accordingly, Catherine does not actively court Peter. Rather she sacrifices her happiness by striving for the unreachable ideal of self-denying virtue. For she feels if Peter wants to be with her he will take the initiative. He will come to her.

Indeed, Catherine takes no action to pursue Keating, since her romantic philosophy in life is sacrificial since it proscribes that it is her duty to wait for the man she loves to come to her. Further, Catherine thinks she may scare Peter away if she is too intense too soon. Accordingly, she does not actively pursue him. Instead she passively waits. And while she waits she tries not to think about Keating too much. But when she does think about him she hopes he will come to her. But when he is away, Catherine misses Peter terribly. But not enough to call him. For she feels that the greater good of their relationship demands that she derive reminiscent pleasure remembering him – while enduring pain as a necessary toll.

In sum, because Catherine does not demand Peter's time he feels comfortable with her. Indeed, he loves her. Not only because Peter feels that with her he is loved for himself but also because he feels he has nothing to gain from Catherine except her love. This is why Peter does not manipulate Catherine to bolster his career, like he does with everyone else. Since he does not want to use and discard her like he does with everyone else.

(2) ANALYSIS OF DOMINIQUE'S SYMBOLIC THOUGH NOT ACTUAL RAPE:

Dominique not only initiates romantic contact with Roark she adamantly pursues him in four ways. First, she gazes at Roark, at the rock quarry, twice, signaling that she wants him. Second, she breaks her fireplace, then summons him to her home, to her bedroom, to fix it, to get him alone, so they can talk. Third, when he arrives, she strikes a seductive pose, at the top of her stairway, inviting him to her boudoir. Fourth, once Roark enters Dominique's bedchamber she persuades him to draw out his time a bit, so that he does rapidly fix the damaged marble slab – with swift practical dispatch – and depart fast. But, rather, takes extra-time to set the marble block, so they get to know each other. To delay him a bit, Dominique says that since she is "paying [Roark] by the hour...it's quite all right if [he] stretches [his] time a little, [since surely] there must be things [he would] like to talk about" (215). Prompted by this invitation, Roark adds time to his job by explaining different types of marble. During their conversation Roark says that "pressure is a powerful factor [since it] leads to consequences which, once started, cannot be controlled..." (216). Although, on the face of it, Roark's comment is only about marble, indirectly, this mention hints at their developing romance. Realizing this Dominique "leans forward" with rapt attention, querying "what consequences?" (216). In reply, Roark tells Dominique to be "very careful" that she choose the right marble for her fireplace, since she does not want "foreign elements [to] infiltrate [from] the surrounding soil" (216). Here, Dominique pays careful attention to the hidden meaning of Roark's veiled reply, since he is not talking *just* about marble. He is hinting that Dominique should also be *very careful* about how she interacts with him. Because her encouragement may have unintended consequences. Brushing off his warning, Dominique insists that Roark set the new marble slab "when it comes" (216).

Clearly the early Rock Quarry and Mansion scenes suggest that Dominique is the main aggressor. For she peruses Roark adamantly.

Dissatisfied with her opening flirtations, however, Dominique's desire for Roark crescendos when she awaits his return. Thus, she hopes that "one of the rare trucks on the road," will deliver her fireplace fixture, so she can interact with Roark again. For she hopes to relieve her "feverish [sexual] intensity," like a bitch in heat, who needs release (217). Ready, then, for playful banter, at the very least, or heterosexual experimentation, at the very most, Dominique snaps "come in" when she thinks Roark is at her door (218). Mortified, however, that Roark sends "a short, squat, middle-aged Italian," man named Pasquale Orsini "to repair [her] fireplace"...Dominique flees from her bedroom to "not be seen by anyone, not...[even] herself" because she wants to hide her desire for Roark from wondering eyes (including her own) because she cannot acknowledge that she the great Dominique Francon wants a modest quarry worker (218, 217). But try as Dominique does to "not go near the quarry," eventually she knows "she [will] go" since Dominique is drawn to Roark like an angel needs light (218). Especially, since she must know why Roark stood her up; why he does not admire her; why he will not yield to her as other men do.

Greatly upset, then, at her ostensible rejection, Dominique gallops to the Quarry atop a charging stallion to ask Roark why he did not fix her fireplace? When she arrives at the pit Roark is not there. He has already finished working. And she knows it. And his absence enrages her further. Until she becomes so frenzied that she bolts into "the woods flying at random [intervals] between walls of leaves" here and walls of leaves there, flurrying about everywhere in a helter-skelter fashion as if her life depended on finding Roark (218). Since Dominique needs to intercept Roark before he gets home, she tears through branches on her steed blazing haphazard trails to find him. Luckily, during her desperate search Dominique sees Roark "walking alone on the path before her," weary after a hard day's work (218). Panting, she asks him "Why he didn't set the marble" slab (218). When Roark replies that he "didn't think it would make any difference to [her] who came. Or, did it Miss Francon?" Dominique lashes him across the face with a denuded tree branch she fashions into a riding crop (218). Her anger, here, suggests that Dominique is wounded, marrow-deep, by Roark's casual brush-off, since she is used to be courted.

Roark's supposed rejection of Dominique not only lowers her feminine pride but also wounds her self-respect, since she thinks she is a great value: a person who should not be scorned by a mere drudge (i.e. a lowly quarry worker) who has no right to spurn her. Humiliated that Roark casts her aside, like a piece of trash, Dominique frets over why he does not want her, since she thinks she can attract any man, especially unsung geniuses. Dominique fails to realize, however, that Roark does like her; he admires her; and is in a way to be in love with her. He only sends Pasquale Orsini to test Dominique's desire for him. To confirm that she wants him. Also by sending Pasquale Orsini, Roark shows Dominique that he holds himself in as much esteem as she does, if not more so, and therefore, he will not automatically yield to her desire to be with him. Her anger at Roark's ostensible jilting, makes him understand how desperately Dominique wants him. So he complies with her desperation.

Later that night, then, after Roark is convinced that Dominique needs to be controlled, he climbs up to her bedroom and takes her by force, thus harnessing her spirit to make her soul give expression to its inner yearnings. Thus, without the slightest trace of mercy Roark corners Dominique with an "austere [look of] cruelty [on his face that expresses the] ascetic [height] of passion, [he feels in his soul]" (219). And though she fights "like an animal," to resist him, "she ma[kes] no sound" (220). Nor, does she "call out for help" when she could have easily stopped Roark's ravishing by screaming for the caretaker (220). But since Dominique thinks that "the act of a master taking shameful, contemptuous possession of her was the kind of rapture she had wanted" she does not yell-out (220). Essentially, because she wants the experience to continue (220). After the deed is done, Dominique never takes a bath since "she want[s] to keep the feeling of [Roark's] body, the traces of his body, on hers, knowing also [that] such [a] desire implied" that she not only liked the experience – on some level – but also that she needed to be overcome by a greater genius (221). Indeed, since Dominique preserves Roark's unique scent; relishes the granite dust from his clothes; glories in the sweaty grim of his body; it is safe to say that her rape was only symbolic, not actual, since if she was truly raped by Roark she would have removed any trace of her rapist's touch from her body to erase her violations memory. But instead of cleansing Roark's scent with a purifying bath, Dominique actually relishes, she actually savors, Roark's smell, because she wants to remember his physical touch on her body, so that she remains connected to him by his odor. Obviously, if Roark really raped Dominique she would not pine for him.

Thus, Roark and Dominique's wild fucking was not rape but something that Dominique wanted to have happen to her since her supposed rape "...was not an actual rape, but a symbolic action which Dominique all but invited [because] this was the action she wanted and Howard Roark knew it" (Michael S. Berliner, ed., Letter of Ayn Rand [New York: Dutton, 1995] 631).

In sum, since Roark knew that Dominique needed to be taken, he took her, thereby creating a situation where they could fall deeply in love and eventually marry—once Dominique accepted his philosophy.

(3) ANALYSIS OF DOMINIQUE'S NON-RELIGIOUS RADIANCE:

In this scene, Dominique radiates a pellucid light from her mind's eye by illuminating her surroundings like a religious saint. But unlike a religious saint, Dominique is an atheist whose glowing halo is not the divine light of a non-existent God. But rather is the radiant nimbus of her mind's eye as transmitted through the stars.

(4) ANALYSIS OF ROARK NOT YIELDING TO DOMINIQUE:

By asking Roark to abandon architecture for loving her, Dominique wants him to exchange his greatest value (architecture) for a lesser value (her), since ultimately, she does not believe that even Roark can forever succeed building his own way: According to his own *sui generis* vision. Since, Dominique thinks that Roark will eventually suffer defeat, at the hands of malevolent actors, in the hard-and-cruel general world, she wants to spare him slow torture a la Henry Cameron. Thus, she urges him to give-up his main purpose—building architectural marvels—to find happiness with her, since she does not think that *even he* is strong enough to forever overcome the onslaughts of critics who denigrate his buildings with their criticism. Thus, Dominique tries to spare Roark the pain of unfair censure, since she cannot endure seeing people distort Roark's life's work. Clearly, Dominique asks Roark to give up architecture not because she is cruel and wants him all to herself. But rather because she wants to spare Roark the inevitable pain of being rejected by rabble who "hate the good for being the good" and thus try to destroy the good to bring them down to their own level. Essentially, Dominique feels that it is better that Roark's soul is euthanized by her loving hands all at once, in one death blow, not slowly broken over 30 years. Ergo, to avert the death of Roark's soul by a thousand pin-pricks Dominique tries to shield him from a hostile society bent on destroying him. Thus, to ensure that Roark is not slowly tortured like Henry Cameron was over three decades, Dominique tries to kill his spirit immediately, in one *coup-de-grace*, so he does not suffer needlessly. Accordingly, she urges Roark to work an unimportant job with unimportant results.

In essence, Dominique tells Roark to give-up architecture in exchange for her love, since she fears that Roark will be destroyed by a pandering public that neither understands his soul like she does, nor appreciates his work like she does, nor recognizes his great human worth like she does, since she knows he is a monumental genius who should be cherished for his unique mind and spotless morality.

By asking Roark to abandon architecture for her, Dominique wants him to accept her own pessimistic philosophy: An ideology that recognizes greatness and appreciates excellence, yet still holds that idealism-and-realism cannot be combined in the real world, since the real world will not allow heroes to flourish indefinitely no matter who they are nor what they do.

In brief, Dominique asks Roark to live *only* for her and she *only* for him, since together she thinks they can be moderately happy. Even if this requires that they give-up their dreams, abandon their souls, and betray the best within them, since it is worth it to her because they will have each other.

But what matters to Roark is architecture. Above all else. Even Dominique. Therefore, in spite of her attempt to persuade him to give-up his career for her, Roark does not abandon building—no matter what she does to undermine his love of architecture—since building is the driving force of his existence. His reason for being. Why he walks the earth. Which he will not leave for anyone. Not even her. Because as important as Dominique is to Roark, what is most important to him is his goal-directed substance. Even more important than her. Thus, Roark will not trade architecture for the passing comforts of a fleeting romance with Dominique, since his love for building supersedes his love for her. Accordingly, Roark curtly dismisses Dominique's odd fancy with a chuckle, telling her that if they lived that kind of empty life she would "soon...beg him to go back to building," since he would be miserable being idle and she would be unhappy seeing her hero debased (483).

(5) ANALYSIS OF HOW DOMINIQUE DISAPPOINTS TOOHEY BY REMAINING CALM:

Toohey tries to upset Dominique by telling her that he cast Roark as an enemy of the people by making him an enemy of religion. That he did this by tricking Roark into designing a radical temple that would violate the values of traditional religion, thereby prompting orthodox religionists to oppose Roark on reactionary grounds. Here, Toohey tries to get a rise out of Dominique by telling her that once the crowd is whipped-up against Roark into a snarling frenzy it will be difficult to fight against them for once an angry public sees red they will not listen to reason. Despite Toohey's challenge to "...fight that my dear when you have no weapons [on your side] except your genius, which is not a weapon but a liability" Dominique remains composed (355). She controls herself throughout since "her eyes [during Toohey's screed are] disappointing; [since] they listen[ed] patiently, [in] an unmoving glance that would not become anger" (356).

(6) ANALYSIS OF WHY WYNAND MARRIES DOMINIQUE:

Though Wynand knows that Dominique does not love him, he is largely unconcerned, since he hopes she will eventually grow to care for him, once she learns who he is. Once she sees his pure inner soul. Therefore, during their courtship – and later marriage – Wynand plays into Dominique's quest to destroy herself for his own private reasons: since he needs to revere a woman with high moral ideals. Thus, he does not object to Dominique using him to numb herself to ethical depravity, since he appreciates her twisted virtue.

(7) ANALYSIS OF DOMINIQUE AND WYNAND'S SIMILARITIES:

Dominique and Wynand are alike in many ways. They both like to amuse themselves by playing with other people's pretense of honor. They both like to tempt others to see if they can either remain honorable – in the face of moral hazard – or gain honor – where they do not have it. Since Dominique and Wynand both like to see how honor operates in other people they share similar characteristics.

(8) ANALYSIS OF KEATING'S LOVE FOR ROARK:

Subconsciously, Keating loves Roark, even though consciously he thinks he hates Roark, since he: values Roark's judgment over others; is proud when Roark praises him in some small way; tells Roark what he truly thinks and feels; confides to Roark his true dreams; fights to defend Roark when people attack him; and, ultimately, thinks Roark is kind, since Roark helps him at school, in his career, and in later life, too.

Evidently, Keating's love for Roark is shown in eight ways.

One, Keating respects Roark's architectural judgment over all other's since he asks Roark whether he should work for Guy Francon in New York or become an arts scholar in Paris—since Roark's "opinion" means more to him than "the Dean's" (21).

Two, when Roark can complement Keating's work in some small way, like "that's not so bad, Peter. You're improving," Keating feels very proud, since he knows that Roark's praise is hard-won and genuine (83).

Three, Keating confides to Roark that he is "never sure" of himself, never quite sure, since Keating needs to learn why Roark always knows what he wants, while Keating never knows (22). Keating's admission here shows readers that he really loves Roark for he would never share his flaws with anyone else except Catherine Halsey who he also loves.

Four, Keating opens up to Roark by showing him his paintings, since he trusts Roark to give him honest feedback about his work, since Roark never tells white-lies to spare people's feelings.

Five, Keating values Roark's schooltime help—at least on some level—since Roark helps him get A's at Stanton, since he "could untangle a plan like pulling a string and it was open." (19). Keating is especially grateful to Roark for fixing his Stanton design projects, since Roark's aid helps him land a job at Francon & Hyer.

Six, Keating also values Roark's design work, since Roark's plans either win him awards, in the case of the Cosmo-Slotnick building prize, or secures him commissions, in the case of the Cortlandt Homes government housing project.

Seven, Keating loves Roark because Roark enables him to win prestige, get fame, earn status, get influence, and make money, which Keating loves—nevermind how he gets these things—since these empty plaudits make Keating feel successful for a while.

Eight, Keating shows his love for Roark when he defends him for designing the Cortlandt Housing Project by asking the public to "leave [Roark] alone, please [to just] leave him alone" (652).

In sum, regardless of the terrible things Keating says about Roark during the story – and in spite of the vicious things he does to him – Roark is Keating's secret "hero, idol, generous friend, and guardian angel" since Keating has "worshiped [Roark] all [his] life...while stabbing him in the back" because Keating loves Roark yet tries to "destroy him." (662). Evidently, all this textual evidence suggests that Roark is Keating's hidden hero – someone to whom he aspires – because Roark is the "kindest man [Keating] know[s]" (608).

(9) ANALYSIS OF TOOHEY BRAINWASHING AND DESTROYING OTHER PEOPLE:

Since Toohey is a Marxist-Communist ideologue he not only disparages the work of maverick architects, like Mr. Durkin, who will not build government housing projects for the masses, he also mocks rich ladies, like Kiki Holcombe, since she hosts lavish parties for wealthy architects, instead of toiling for peasants. In fact Toohey pours scorn on these two individuals since he cannot fully control them. Since he cannot make one man build to his uniform building standards nor the other woman fit neatly into his new world order.

In general, Toohey traduces people he cannot rule to subvert their independence, so they become a plaything in his hands ready for molding: mindless automatons who will do whatever he says. But if people do not go along with his plans Toohey publicly maligns their standing by insulting their characters, undercutting their work, and questioning their professional purpose, so that either they abandon their beliefs to him entirely, or suffer public ostracism for opposing him. Thus, by unleashing a stunning barrage of psychological attacks against people he cannot fully control, Toohey breaks people's spirits, dominates their wills, and controls their minds, so they yield. So they buckle to his will. So they voluntarily fill themselves with the ideas Toohey wants them to contain.

(10) ANALYSIS OF TOOHEY'S FORESHADOWING:

Toohey foreshadows that his identity—i.e. what moves him to act—is largely a mystery wrapped inside a riddle delivered through an enigma, which most characters do not understand at first.

By the end of the novel, however, readers discover that Toohey does not help people, he harms them. That he is not a saint as most people think he is but rather is a menace to society. That though Toohey pretends to be a humanitarian who uplifts people with idealism really he is a wolf in sheep's clothing who only fakes benevolence to hide his inner danger. A person who will metastasize into a virulent form of cancer (especially if left unchecked) that will first cripple then kill a healthy organism. That really Toohey is not so innocent after all, even though he pretends to be idealistic.

Essentially, Toohey builds reader suspense about his secret nature by making a series of bizarre statements in the story. These comments suggest he is not what he seems. That he is not benevolent. That when the time is right he will shed his cloak of respectability to reveal that he is not what he pretends to be but much worse. Further, all the dark hints about Toohey scattered throughout the novel stokes readers to discover what Toohey is really after? What he is really about? What makes Toohey tick? Why Toohey is how he is? What makes him do what he does? Eventually, readers discover that the mystery behind Toohey's dark hints about himself is resolved near the end of the book, when Toohey strongarms Keating.

During his final speech to Keating readers learn just how evil Toohey is when he confesses to: destroying architecture by building-up Peter Keating; destroying literature by building-up Lois Cook; destroying the press by building-up Lancelot Clokey; and destroying the theater by building-up Ike. Readers also learn from Toohey's speech that when he attacks other people's values he does so to make them feel unworthy to make serious decisions. So they rely on his counsel.

(11) ANALYSIS OF HOW TOOHEY SEEKS TO CONTROL OTHERS BY PREACHING ARCHITECTURAL UNIFORMITY:

Toohey recommends strict adherence to classicism, without creativity, without originality, without inventiveness, without uniqueness, so he can bundle one more category of people—one more social grouping of citizens—into yet another monolith of humans he can control. So that one more segment of society is ready for him to slip a leash-of-rule around their necks. So that he can add one more collection of people to the long list of folks he already rules. Until he rules them all. Until he unites the globe into a communist dictatorship, where everyone sacrifices to everyone and everyone is equally miserable. A worldwide proletariat where his iron fist is forced onto billions.

Thus, by advocating uniform block buildings that conform to classical building canons, Toohey backs not an inventive creativity signaling the independence of an architect to conceive new and significant designs. But rather he urges architects to simply imitate – to merely regurgitate – past building traditions by modeling their work on former building styles. So that architects are not pioneering spirits that blaze new paths with their original buildings thereby inspiring the earth with a new spirit of modern progress. But instead are made pliable by being shackled to what has been done before. Thus, by advocating architectural monotony Toohey not only tries to tear humanity back to a previous and worse condition but also by promoting building sameness Toohey tries to homogenize all people, regardless of difference, so he can rule them all, easily, without challenge. Ergo, it is no surprise that he measures the repeating design features of buildings as a touchstone to the universizability of all architecture, because he wants domiciles and their builders to be identical in form and equal in substance, too. So he can control them all.

In fact, Toohey's advocacy of monotonous block buildings reminds me of the drab appearance of Moscow's state-owned housing tenements, which are characterized by row-after-row of rambling residences without marked differences: dull, dreary, and depressing.

(12) ANALYSIS OF WHY WYNAND RAISES TOOHEY'S SALARY INSTEAD OF FIRING HIM:

Wynand raises Toohey's salary not because he supports Toohey's labor union stance – he finds it abhorrent – but because Toohey is an effective rabble-rouser, a "good booby trap," who helps him transmogrify public fervor into mass hysteria by rousing public controversy into full-frenzy, so he can sell more newspapers (521). Therefore, once the public sees red, Wynand cashes in on the furor that Toohey stirs for him by writing outlandish articles that further tap into the passions and prejudices of the people (521). And since growing *The Banner's* circulation is Wynand's ultimate aim he hires demagogues like Toohey to pluck at the heart strings of the common man by posing as the champion of everyman. And since Toohey's controversy helps Wynand sell more newspapers he rewards Toohey with a fitting raise for his rhetoric, since Toohey's sensationalism helps Wynand make money. In sum, because money is power to Wynand, Wynand thinks that Toohey's demagoguery will enable him to make more money and thus gain more power over people, thereby heightening the populist appeal of his media empire. This, then, is why Wynand is elated by Toohey's labor speech, since he thinks Toohey's hullabaloo will not only enable him to extort more money from New Yorkers but his hubbub will also allow him to win more power over New York City, so he can gather tighter and tighter reigns of control into his hands until he runs everything.

(13) ANALYSIS OF HOW WYNAND USES EXPEDIENT IDEOLOGIES TO MAKE MONEY AND GAIN POWER:

To consolidate his rule over people, Wynand uses whatever ideology is popular at the moment, even Marxist communism, since his end goal is to sell more copies of the *Banner*, not to produce and disseminate moral values. Accordingly, Wynand even embraces anti-capitalist ideologies, like world communism, for instance, because he relies on a herd of unthinking zombies to fuel his lust for power: so he grows more potent in the short term, even though he destroys himself in the long term. Thus, instead of promoting world capitalism (which incidentally made him rich in the first place) Wynand panders to momentary public trends (whatever they may be) by depending on ideologues, like Toohey, to generate public sentiment for him, so that he can extract people's money.

Yet, by abetting Toohey, Wynand nurtures the very force that destroys him.

(14) ANALYSIS OF HOW TOOHEY CONTROLS PEOPLE BY DIVIDING THEM AGAINST THEMSELVES:

Toohey degrades the best within men by brainwashing people into believing that they need a ruler like him to tell them what to think, how to act, and what to pursue. Part of this brainwashing process entails turning people against themselves through a process of internal corruption, until nothing remains sacred to them.

(15) ANALYSIS OF TOOHEY'S LONELINESS:

Since Toohey needs people to recognize, understand, appreciate, identify with, and witness him, he tries to confide in various characters throughout the novel. So he does not feel all alone. People who not only understand Toohey for who he is but also appreciate him for what he wants. Ultimately, however, Toohey is frustrated in his search for someone to comprehend him, since he cannot talk to Alvah Scarret or Gus Web because they wouldn't understand. The only person he admires (on some level) is Dominique Francon who at least classifies Toohey for who he is not what he pretends to be.

(16) ANALYSIS OF HOW TOOHEY TURNS PEOPLE INTO HIS SLAVES:

Toohey is a master psychological manipulator who persuades people to believe what he wants them to believe so ultimately they become his slaves. But to gain control of people's souls he first has to drain individuals of all their personal values. So they do not oppose him with thoughts of their own, emotions of their own, a will of their own, or a mind of their own. So eventually they become his lackeys who will empower him by voting him into office.

Indeed Toohey looks forward to seizing the bully pulpit of the presidency so he can order people around without consoling them, once he controls the guns. Yet until that dark day Toohey is resigned to kill men's souls on a spiritual level by dividing men against themselves on a psychological one, thereby rendering them social tofu with no distinct flavor of their own only a taste that Toohey gives them.

In this regard, Toohey's basic strategy is to first seize the reigns of political power by grooming a legion of stupefied followers. Then, once he converts people to his sway, Toohey places his yes men in positions of minor bureaucratic influence all over the country, so he can leverage them as a stepping-stone to rise to wider-and-wider levels of power: until, one day, he is strong enough to be voted into office, where he will then transmogrify the American constitutional system – based on freedom and individualism – into a tyrannical communist dictatorship, where his fiats will be enforced by a slew of his political henchman, like the thuggish Gus Webb, for instance.

In brief, Toohey sees the manipulation of people as a necessary evil to seize control of the presidency (at least in an advisory capacity) so he can rule the military, the police force, and the machinery of the deep-state by proxy, thereby becoming a physical killer, not just a spiritual one.

(17) ANALYSIS OF HOW KEATING BETRAYS ROARK BECAUSE HE IS AFRAID OF TOOHEY:

While Toohey *seems* to be Keating's friend, really he primes Keating for a hostile takeover by not only destroying all of his values—such as his love for Catherine Halsey, for example—but also by eradicating any trace of architectural integrity he may have once had. He does this by not only mocking love in general but also by having him chair the *Council of American Architects*, which is an organization designed to destroy all American architectural values. Here, Toohey's schemes not only undercut Keating's love for Catherine his plots also undermine Keating's pride in designing at least halfway decent buildings. Further, by prompting him to design an ugly building for Lois Cook Toohey weakens Keating's esthetic design principles further. In sum, by emptying Keating's soul of his personal values, such as his love for a woman, and by draining Keating's desire to build buildings that are esthetically pleasing, Toohey controls Keating by first voiding any principles he has. Then filling the void of his interiority with ideas Toohey wants his soul to contain. Evidently, because Keating falls victim to Toohey's schemes, he becomes his lackey, which is evident when we consider that he betrays Roark to Toohey by telling him that Roark designed Cortlandt.

Evidently, Keating is so cowed by Toohey's badgering that he soon yields to Toohey's merciless onslaught of words: offering only token resistance (at first) which soon melts away under the heat of Toohey's persistent hounding. Afraid of what Toohey might inflict on him if he does not give-in – if he does not buckle – Keating's psychological resistance to his machinations finally gives way. It crumbles. To the extent that Keating betrays Roark to him by turning over their Cortlandt contract. Ultimately, Keating's betrayal of Roark shows readers that he will do anything for Toohey when this arch-villain squeezes him.

Keating suddenly developing the moxie to defy and defeat Toohey during the final hour—when he has been Toohey's lapdog for over 10 years—would be highly illogical, since he cannot suddenly unwind his psychological dependence on Toohey overnight, since Keating has followed his guidance for most of his adult life. Thus, even though Keating knows Toohey for what he really is (i.e. someone who has destroyed his soul) he still follows Toohey. He'll "never be able to leave [Toohey because he] has obeyed [Toohey] in the name of ideals. [Therefore he'll] go on obeying [Toohey] without ideals because that is all [Keating's] good for now" (670).

(18) ANALYSIS OF TOOHEY'S FINAL DEFEAT:

By the end of the book Toohey is defeated in all of his major goals. He cannot stop Roark from becoming a prominent architect. He cannot jail Roark for exploding Cortlandt. He is unable to rule the *Banner* after 13 years of incessant scheming. By the end of the story, the substance of Toohey's energy is already spent, since at age 65 he no longer has the time to gain the power he seeks, even though he will try on the *Courier*.

(19) ANALYSIS OF HOW WYNAND LOOKS AND BEHAVES LIKE MEPHISTOPHELES2:

According to Wikipedia Mephistopheles is a demon featured in German Folklore who is trapped in his own self-made hell, since he sold his soul for money and power. Wynand, like Mephistopheles, is also trapped in his own self-made hell, since he betrayed the best within him for riches and authority.

(20) ANALYSIS OF WYNAND'S SUICIDAL TENDENCIES:

Because Wynand feels empty inside for betraying his soul, he thinks, often, about committing suicide, since the blank routine of his perfunctory life—which consists of overseeing the *Banner*, talking emptily at meetings, and copulating with shallow yet beautiful women— disgusts him to the point that he does not see a reason to live. Yet he thinks that suicide should only be committed – if it must – out of some extreme passion, "either a great joy, or a healthy terror" (405). Accordingly, he believes that to shoot himself for no good reason is not the way to end his life, since a person should treat suicide as a solemn act performed with great seriousness.

(21) ANALYSIS OF HOW WYNAND'S PRIVATE ART GALLERY EXPRESSES HIS SOUL:

Wynand's private art gallery is a sanctuary for his soul – a physical refuge for his body – which makes him feel young again, since just visiting

---

[2] Mephistopheles: By Mark Antokolski, 1884.

Since Mephistopheles appears to Faustus as a demon – a worker for Lucifer – critics claim that he damns people's souls. In this connection, Mephistopheles walks the earth trying to tempt and corrupt any virtuous man he encounters because he wants them to join him in his own private hell.

his art gallery causes Wynand to view human beings not as depraved creatures huddling together in benighted darkness but as people capable of creating artistry of high intellectual, moral, and spiritual worth. Accordingly, simply contemplating his art gallery refreshes Wynand's soul with a vision of man's greatness, so he looks and feels 20 years younger.

(22) ANALYSIS OF WYNAND'S WORK ROUTINE:

To manage his media conglomerate, Wynand edits articles, gives speeches, and engages in sundry activities by day. Then, at night he sleeps four hours, often waking early in the morning to review important articles from his newspapers, magazines, and books, from New York City, Philadelphia, Springville Kansas, and elsewhere. After making shorthand notes that only a trusted secretary can decipher, Wynand goes to the office for yet another full day of work. This, then, is the routine Wynand follows for most of the year, when he is not vacationing on his yacht.

(23) ANALYSIS OF THE DISCONNECT BETWEEN WYNAND'S OUTER VULGARITY AND HIS INNER PURITY:

People cannot understand how a man, like Wynand, who runs a corrupt media empire, like Wynand enterprises, can have the esthetic judgment to purchase an exquisite penthouse of such rare simplicity and splendid beauty, so utterly opposed to the gross demagoguery of his newspapers. Indeed, people are so stupefied by the disconnect between Wynand's beautiful private residence and his sordid public ugliness that they ogle in bewilderment at his penthouse, since they are stunned by the difference between his excellent private judgment and his horrendous public pandering. But despite people's breathless admiration for Wynand's remarkable penthouse they cannot express *total* enthusiasm for his residence on moral grounds. Because Wynand is an evil monster to them – a base scoundrel who they cannot admire for any reason whatsoever, even though he is renowned for having the esthetic sensibilities of a master artist.

In sum, even though Wynand belies the *Banner's* sordid disvalues with the splendor of his personal possessions—such as his private art gallery, for example, or his country home and yacht, for instance—people cannot reconcile the vast discrepancy between Wynand's private inner soul and his public outer persona (i.e. who he is in private and what he writes in print).

(24) ANALYSIS OF WHY WYNAND IS UNHAPPY DESPITE HIS SEEMING SUCCESS:

Though Wynand is a media mogul who owns various newspapers, magazines, and radio stations—and though he is a real estate tycoon who owns many different buildings, corporations, and subsidiaries, Wynand's power over information streams does not make him happy, his ownership of many different properties does not bring him joy, his ability to fornicate with gorgeous yet empty women does not fulfill him spiritually, since he knows he got all these things by graft, corruption, and, above all, by creating and disseminating public disvalues. For this reason, he feels utterly base – even though he is a complete success in conventional eyes – since he knows (if only subconsciously) that he betrayed himself to make money dishonestly.

(25) ANALYSIS OF WYNAND'S POSSESSIVENESS:

Since Wynand cherishes the people and possessions he loves, such as Dominique Francon, for example, or his private art gallery, for instance, or Howard Roark, case in point, he protects them from the outside world.

Concomitantly, he turns Dominique's bedroom from a glass cube visible to all of Manhattan into a metal vault safe from prying eyes. Similarly, he protects his private art gallery by locating it in a windowless chamber on the 52nd floor of his private penthouse safe from the intrusive gaze of others. With both Dominique and his art gallery Wynand hermetically seals the spaces in which they are housed, so they are not defiled by toxic outside air, since he must shelter them from corrupt external influences. He must protect Dominique from New York City since she is his queen who he does not want to see degraded. He must protect his art gallery from New York City since his art collection expresses his inner soul which cannot be shared. Similarly, since Wynand loves Roark he wishes he could feed him at the Nordland Hotel as if Roark were actually broke and really needed the meal, since he wants to make Roark healthy and strong. In fact Wynand loves Roark so much that he wants to cruise with him, on the high seas, all alone, so he does not have to share him with anyone.

(26) ANALYSIS OF HOW WYNAND FEEDS OFF OF THE PUBLIC THROUGH THE BANNER:

By churning out *maudlin* articles for decades – writings that express people's worst side – Wynand spreads human depravity daily, by showing people that they are benighted creatures subject to the sudden ups-and-downs (or vicissitudes) of viceful emotional floundering. Indeed, because people (to Wynand) are mishapen souls screaming from the edge of a sordid flesh-pit, they inexorably lust for depravity daily, since perversion is an ineluctable part of the human condition. For evil, to Wynand, is what makes the world go round. It is what makes a person tick. Therefore, to fight sordidness (as most people do) is futile to Wynand, since he believes that depravity is an inescapable feature of the murky human psyche. Thus, Wynand feels he must indulge his readers dark sides with daily articles of vice and corruption: writings that enable them to swallow evil wholesale, since it is sugarcoated with a hollow mask of virtue. A thin veneer of idealism, if you will, that crumbles away on close inspection. Indeed, since Wynand wants to enrich and empower himself by feeding off of others sores he produces lurid stories everyday: narratives that show people their darker devils while obscuring their brighter angels. He does this by writing sentimental stories that appeal to people's passions and prejudices; so he can deliver people's inevitable vices to them.

Indeed, to Wynand the creation of the *Banner* is simply an enterprising move. It is just plain good horse sense, since everybody has to make a living. Nevermind that his *Banner* expresses the worst within people. Wynand does not care. He only cares about wresting money and power from civilization. Thus, he does not feel guilty for crafting garish stories that generate, sustain, and perpetuate the basest disvalues possible to man, since he feels that people can only rise in this way.

Wynand's constant demagoguery, however, instead of making him happy for gaining a leg-up on others (i.e. instead of making him feel proud for being clever enough to extract money and power from society) actually makes him miserable, much of the time, because Wynand knows – at least on some level – that he has betrayed the best within him by pandering to the masses. Accordingly, Wynand questions if he was right to sell his soul for copious amounts of money, since trading his innocence for power is a pyric victory offset by the staggering loss of his being. Wynand soon realizes, however, that the cost of his immoral drive for status are depressed feelings of doom-and-gloom (i.e. frequent bouts of suicidal depression).

But because Wynand would rather rule the herd then be a victim of it (i.e. since he would rather be a strong man then a mindless sheep) he justifies his evil media empire by deluding himself into believing that the ends justify the means. That since people are inherently wicked anyway he might as well get rich and powerful feeding off their inevitable vices. That to not benefit from people's evil would be foolish. Accordingly, Wynand provides a forum for people to indulge their vices before someone else does. So he can get rich off of other people's suffering.

Since Wynand's life philosophy is that people are either rulers who control the masses or followers who take orders from the masses he is eager to rule the *hoi pollio* not be ruled by the *hoi pollio*, since he wants to control the flock not be controlled by the flock. Said differently, because Wynand wants to be a shepherd who herds and fleeces his human sheep not a mindless sheep who follows the dictates of a ruling shepherd, he is eager to aggrandize himself by exploiting human suffering. Not by being a human sufferer himself. This is why Wynand strives to be a strong man who forces others to obey his orders – not a weak man who follows others orders – by not only broadcasting gloomy ideas of a dystopian world where man cannot help but be depraved but also by promoting the basest disvalues imaginable in print through his yellow scandal rags.

(27) ANALYSIS OF WHY WYNAND'S STAFF ARE AFRAID OF HIM:

Though Wynand is polite to his employees, pays them above average salaries and chooses the best talents he can find, his workers are afraid of him for two reasons. One, they do not want to be fired by him. Two, they do not want to be hurt by him.

First, Wynand's employees are terrified of him because they do not want to be fired by him for insubordination, since they depend on their *Banner* jobs to pay rent, buy food, and purchase the goods and services they need to survive. Consequently, they cower at the prospect of being canned by Wynand since he often fires people on-the-spot – for any reason or no reason at all – often without severance. He does this to Ellsworth Toohey, for example. Or Allen and Falk, for instance. Thus, Wynand's employees feel they must obey his strictures precisely, without question, since everyone is expendable to Wynand. Even employees who have worked for him for years. For example, Sally Brent is immediately nixed for writing a story on Dominique Wynand, since she countermands Wynand's standing order to not write articles about his wife. Evidently, Wynand is to be obeyed by his employees without question, since he is willing to fire anyone who does not follow his marching orders to a tee – including a seasoned staffer whose departure means the loss of many readers. In brief, even though Wynand knows that he will lose a large *Banner* following with Sally Brent's sacking he issues a security directive to never let her in the building again anyway since it is Wynand's way or the highway on his daily *Banner*.

Second, Wynand's staffers are petrified that if they disobey him— either knowingly or unknowingly, consciously or unconsciously—he will bloody them for getting in his way, since he either injures workers who talk back to him or threatens employees with violence if they express opinions he does not like. For instance, Wynand throws a new hire bodily down "two flights of stairs," for getting cheeky with him, breaking his "ankle" in the process. (677) He also threatens Alvah Scarret with the gruesome prospect of getting " 'his teeth...bash[ed] in' " if he does not keep still (652). Since it is no *Stretch* of the imagination for Wynand's employees to envision him becoming violent with them – since he regularly punched people's lights out when he was a dockyard bully – Wynand's workers remain motionless in his presence, since they are afraid that their boss will mash their faces in for displeasing him. To avoid being victimized by his violence, then, Wynand's employees only interact with him when they must. At other times they keep away from him. Even if it means working overtime.

In sum, since Wynand's employees do not want to be fired for insubordination – or injured for getting in Gail's way – they carry out his instructions with military discipline.

(28) ANALYSIS OF WYNAND'S GANGSTERLIKE IMPULSES:

Like most Manhattan gangsters, Wynand grabs power on the mean streets of New York City by pummeling his targets into submission. Until he forces his victims to do his bidding. Yet when he becomes the head of an evil media empire bent on world-wide domination Wynand finds he can no longer solve his problems by punching people anymore. He also finds that he can no longer bend reality to his will by throttling folks as he once did when he was a Hell's Kitchen guttersnipe, since the business world will not permit him to achieve his goals by gore.

Evidently, Wynand discovers that because the world of journalism is populated by editors, writers, copy men, photographers, and slot men, not murders, sneak thieves, grafters, card sharks, and prostitutes, the street-gore he formerly used as a gangster—to rise from a wharf-rat to a dockyard-king—will not work in a corporate setting. Accordingly, Wynand abandons the carnage of his *erstwhile* strongarm bully tactics so he can lead a media conglomerate to financial success. Ergo, to gain power over the media business, Wynand uses brains not muscles – intelligence not brawn – to win fiduciary rewards, since nuance is needed to win prominence in the newspaper business. Not physical force.

Make no mistake, though, despite Wynand's sophisticated polish, graceful charm, and winsome manners, he is still a gangster at heart. Because even though the outward form of his predation has changed from robbing people's material goods to robbing people's spiritual values he still exploits others. He still steps all over them to get what he wants. He still steals from people, metaphorically, by persuading them to surrender their souls to him. Thus, to brainwash his readers into accepting whatever he writes, Wynand bombards them with hyper-emotional stories on a daily basis. Until his hyperbolic articles distorts people's characters to the degree that he can easily steal their values through his newspaper. Since, by publishing corrupt stories, they are independent no longer. Now, they depend on him to tell them what to think.

As head of Wynand Enterprises, then, what has changed are the weapons Wynand uses to steal from people. Not the strategy he deploys to drain money from them. For now Wynand controls people through the media (i.e. through the might of his bottomless checkbook) not fists, knives, or guns anymore. This, then, is how he shifts his target from goods of the body to goods of the soul by swapping physical force for mental coercion.

Indeed, now that Wynand owns a media empire, he either restrains himself when he wants to use violence, to control the scene, or he allows himself to be restrained by his friends, since *sometimes* he needs their help to calm down. Textually this is evident when Wynand suppresses his bouts of fury with Roark's help. To explain, when Wynand sees Roark enjailed for exploding Cortlandt he is murderously angry. So upset that he is ready to blow up the jail and attack the officers holding Roark. If Roark was not there to tranquilize Wynand he may have tried. But because Roark soothes him, first from his jail cell, with gentle speech, then by leading Wynand by his hand to his car, Wynand overmasters his trembling fury. Yet sometimes Wynand controls his violent emotions himself without anyone's help. On his own. Like when he suppresses his anger when *The Banner*'s managing editor tells him that other journalists, such as Toohey, Faulk, Allen and Harding *may* also have truth on their side. Instead of bashing Scarret's teeth in right then-and-there as he might have done before, Wynand breaks his fit-of-anger, in midstream, to conduct business as usual.

These examples prove that on one level Wynand knows that violence can no longer be used to accomplish his goals. On another level, Wynand is tempted to revert to his former gangster ways, since he is accustomed to forcing men to do what he wants through bodily compulsion. By beating them up. In the end, though, Wynand overcomes his gangland impulses, on multiple occasions, to restore his tranquility of mind and emotions.

Now he calmly relies on controlling the flow of information to navigate his way to money and power (not beating people up anymore) since the playing field has now changed. Now the map has transformed from a rough-and-tumble layout of city streets—with gruesome corridors, blind alleys, and underground sewers—to a luxurious layout of glass towers, airconditioned offices, and well-lit conference rooms. In this setting, Wynand uses constructive reason, not destructive rage, to accomplish his goals, because here one must persuade people to follow their will by being rational: not by hitting them over the head until they submit. In other words, Wynand now realizes that he must deal in thought to achieve his aims—not force to ram his will down people's throats. Thus, as head of Wynand Enterprises Wynand uses persuasion to convince people to follow him – not physical force anymore.

In brief, although Wynand is a strong man with extraordinary self-control he has to exercise great equanimity when he suffers bouts of rage, so he does not use the gore he once did when he was a gang leader. This is probably because Wynand realizes – on some level – that getting over-upset, then violent, for a perceived injustice will not help him achieve his goals. For he now realizes, perhaps subconsciously, that anger is a form of weakness that precludes him from acting rationally.

(29) ANALYSIS OF WYNAND'S BITTER HAPPINESS AT BEING BEATEN BY ROARK:

Wynand is both happy and sad to be beaten by Roark. Happy that pure individuals with incorruptible souls like Roark exist, since Roark shows him an innocent vision of the world and man's place in it. Sad because Roark's success shows him how far his rotten personality has fallen from the tree of life; from the ideal of perfection. That though it was possible for him to be a first-hander (a first-rater) who succeeded in life by using his creative genius he became a second-hander (a second-rater) who feeds off of the disfigurements of humanity. On one hand, Wynand is happy that Roark flourishes through the substance of his ideas not the consensus of other people. On the other hand, Wynand feels chastised by Roark's life, since Roark rises by creating and fostering individual architectural values, while Wynand rises by originating and nurturing collective media vice.

In brief, though Wynand is happy that Roark inspires him with the hope to succeed in life because of his virtues and perfections not in spite of them, he is still saddened that Roark reminds him of what he could have been, should have been, but did not have the strength to be, since Wynand chose to pervert his moral soul by banking off of suffering and death, instead of building his moral character by promoting life and living.

In conclusion, though Wynand is pained by the recognition that he could have been like Roark, should have been like Roark, but did not become like Roark he is happy that success is still possible for men like Roark despite what the world throws at them.

(30) ANALYSIS OF HOW WYNAND TRIES TO BE LIKE ROARK:

Though Roark is like Wynand in many ways (i.e. they both grew-up poor, worked many different odd-jobs, and are self-made successes) he is the best of Wynand without his corruptions. Without his vices. For he choose to become successful by adhering to firm principles, while

Wynand prostituted his soul for money and power. Yet Roark's success inspires Wynand to become a better man since Roark's achievements show him that *real* success is possible for first-handers. Accordingly, Roark prompts Wynand to overcome himself by transcending his vice-ridden outer self to embrace his health-giving inner being, by modeling his soul on Roark's example. Thus, by drawing energy from Roark's revitalizing essence, Wynand suggests that he too may evolve to Roark's level in time. If he tries hard enough. For Wynand believes that what one man can do another can do, especially if two men are alike in many intrinsic ways despite having extrinsic differences. Accordingly, Wynand needs to be with Roark so he can learn from Roark. So he can fuel his mind, evolve his emotions, and purify his essence, with Roark's counterbalancing example. This is why Wynand frees Roark, defends Roark, feeds Roark, cruises with Roark, and visits Roark. So he has the necessary exposure to be like Roark.

(31) ANALYSIS OF HOW TOOHEY HARMS WYNAND AND WHY WYNAND LETS HIM:

Though Wynand thwarts Toohey's hostile takeover of the *Banner* by closing his top publication, Toohey effectively cripples Wynand's corrupt media empire by corroding his flagship newspaper. So Toohey can run things himself. So he can wrangle control of the *Banner* as a step to controlling Wynand's radio, print, and television syndicate. To do this, Toohey takes a number of actions. First, he convinces the *Banner's* employees to strike. Second, he compels people to boycott the *Banner* by orchestrating the *We Don't Read Wynand* campaign. Third, he arranges for the *Banner's* sponsors to stop advertising in the newspaper. Fourth he persuades Mitchell Layton to buy a large hunk of the *Banner*, so his lackey can eventually buy Wynand out. Eventually, all of Toohey's actions against the *Banner* pressures Wynand to either rehire Toohey and reform the *Banner's* editorial policy or run an unbought, unread, newspaper, at a staggering financial loss. But instead of handing over control of his darling newspaper to Toohey, Wynand fires him, closes the

Banner, and cripples his media empire. He does this because he cannot bear to see Toohey take-over his *Banner*. Because he created it – not Toohey. Thus, to avoid becoming a figurehead who follows Toohey's marching orders, Wynand shuts his leading newspaper, since he can not stand to see himself relegated to a mere figurehead, while Toohey becomes the real power behind his throne.

With the daily *Banner* closed all that remains of Wynand's broadcasting empire in New York City is a small tabloid named the *Clarion*, which aggregates smutty human interest stories mostly of a dubious nature. Besides this yellow scandal rag, Wynand's media presence in New York City is essentially dead. But elsewhere he is alive and kicking, since Wynand still owns prominent newspapers in other major cities, like the *Philadelphia Star* in Philadelphia Pennsylvania, for example, or the *Springville Wynand Herald* in Springville Kansas, for instance. But even though Wynand owns healthy media organs in other locales, the beating heart of his broadcast syndicate stops pumping because of Toohey.

In the final analysis Wynand falls victim to Toohey's depredations since he never understands Toohey's motives (i.e. why he does what he does) because he feels it is a waste of his time to dissect Toohey's moral character. Therefore, Wynand never discovers Toohey's ultimate goal – which is global domination – since Wynand thinks that contemplating Toohey is not necessary. This is why Wynand ignores Dominique's two dire warnings that Toohey is trying to take over his daily *Banner*. Unaware of the danger of losing control of his media conglomerate, Wynand allows Toohey to organize a labor union on his paper, since he sees no threat in such a harmless organization.

Ironically, Wynand hires and supports the very person who destroys him. He does this for two reasons: One, to increase the *Banner's* circulation by attracting Toohey's public to his masthead. And, two, to heighten his influence by using Toohey's populist rhetoric in his newspaper. But here Wynand underestimates Toohey capacity for evil, since he does not think that understanding him is important.

In brief, because Wynand gravely underestimates Toohey's ability to take-over his daily *Banner*, he loses control of his top newspaper, which eventually precipitates the death of the rest of his media empire, which will fail after Wynand's life.

(32) ANALYSIS OF WYNAND'S DEFENSE OF ROARK OVER THE CORTLANDT DYNAMITING:

Because Wynand cannot tolerate seeing Roark besmirched in print over the Cortlandt dynamiting he offers to hire the entire legal profession to free Roark, since he cannot bear to see his friend's freedom taken away. Further, Wynand defends Roark – in the court of public opinion – by penning a variety of articles that paint him in a favorable light. As either the victim of the government housing project racket, or as a creative talent that should be appreciated, or as an innocent man who should not be judged guilty before his trial.

(33) ANALYSIS OF WHY WYNAND CANNOT DEFEND ROARK WITH THE BANNER:

When Wynand tries to defend Roark over the Cortlandt dynamiting he realizes that he cannot suddenly change the nature of a corrupt media instrument like the *Banner* – which he has used to destroy people's values for decades – into a source of clean broadcast journalism overnight: for he learns that it is impossible to turn a collective mob of degraded people who are out for blood into a group of civilized individuals who recognize virtue and value reason. On the contrary, Wynand learns that the forces of the *status quo*, which he has supported for over 10 years, will push back hard against him if he suddenly tries to change his editorial policy.

Further, Wynand discovers that his readers do not want to be given values. Rather, they want to read perverted stories, on a daily basis, about how wicked humanity is, to excuse their moral depravity. Since these kinds of lurid stories make them feel better about themselves, since it excuses their vices by convincing them that everyone is corrupt. That they cannot help but be wicked.

Therefore, when Wynand tries to appeal to his readers' sense of fairness to defend Roark he experiences public blowback in the form of people boycotting his newspaper, picketing in front of his office, causing property damage, destroying copies of The *Banner*, and even sending his writers to the hospital. Sadly, this trauma teaches Wynand that he cannot suddenly introduce a healthy editorial policy on the *Banner*—when its' readers are used to sensationalism—for when the *Banner's* readers do not get the stories they expect of Wynand they tear him down.

In sum, after being gobbled-up by the *Banner* for trying to defend the good for being the good, Wynand realizes that he does not rule the public. That they rule him. That without the public's support he would never have made so much money or gained so much power.

(34) ANALYSIS OF THE SIMILARITY BETWEEN WEBB'S PERSONALITY & A TOILET:

Gus Webb's toxic personality suits building johns exactly. Because like toilets collect repulsive human waste (i.e. excrement, urine, and throw-up) his personality is a human cesspool of raw sewage that gathers and stores people's refuse. Yet, while people can flush-out a toilet's impurities by depressing a lever, Webb cannot sanitize his toxic character quickly (if at all) by his own human agency, since his personality is a stagnant cesspit of human putridification.

(35) ANALYSIS OF WHY FOUGLER HATES WEBB:

Fougler hates Webb for three reasons. One, he hates Webb because Webb "doesn't understand literature [since to him] it's a nonproductive" waste of time (485). Two he hates Webb because Webb advocates for the "liquidat[ion] of authors" in a future Marxist government (485). Three he hates Webb because Webb's sloppiness grates on Fougler's sensibilities, since Fougler "never gags [because it's] "vulgar" (486). Since it is natural to *detest* someone who thinks your profession is bosh, who wants to kill the people you depend on to live, and who reviles you with their slackness, it is obvious why Fougler hates Webb. Because when someone tells crude jokes, mocks your livelihood, and wishes to exterminate your patrons, the natural reaction is to dislike this person strongly.

(36) ANALYSIS OF HOW TOOHEY DESCENDS TO WEBB'S GROSS LEVEL TO NOT ONLY CONTROL HIM BUT ALSO TO CONTROL OTHERS THROUGH HIM:

Toohey descends to Webb's primitive conceptual level by exploiting bawdy jokes, making randy references, uttering vulgar slang, and intoning informal colloquialisms, since this sloppy talk makes Webb feel that Toohey understands him. That Toohey is like him. That Toohey and he can abet each other to realize their Marxist goals, since they both share smutty minds, characterized by uncouth speech. Thus, to convince Webb that they should be partners-in-crime, Toohey charms him by appealing to his gross sense of humor, all by pretending to speak like him and think like him. So that Webb does what Toohey wants him to do, by speaking "with old Bassett" not with his usual abrasive style but with a milder, gentler approach, so that old Bassett does what Webb tells him to do, which is ultimately what Toohey wants him to do (472). In brief, by instructing Webb to sooth his confederates with comforting speech, Toohey uses him as an intermediary to control others. So that people do what Toohey wants done through Webb.

(37) ANALYSIS OF HOW FRANCON TAKES CREDIT FOR OTHER PEOPLE'S WORK:

Though the firm of Francon & Hyer builds 31 buildings, Guy Francon only designed 2 of them: *The Frink National Bank Building* and the *Melton Building*. But he takes credit for 29 other buildings by delegating the designing and drafting of these structures to his head designer Claude Stengel and his favored draftsmen Tim Davis, while counting on his minor staff to work out the details. When these buildings are finished, he affixes his signature to the final product, thereby taking credit for their work.

Since Francon stopped designing and drafting new buildings long ago he not only relies on the prestige of his old buildings to flourish he also depends on his employee's new buildings to succeed. Nowadays his only role is wining and dining clients, giving talks at banquets, recruiting new prospects, like Peter Keating, to work for him. And once Francon hires Peter Keating like people he takes credit for their work by signing his name to their buildings, as if he designed them, when he did not.

(38) ANALYSIS OF HOW GUY FRANCON & PETER KEATING ARE DIFFERENT AND ALIKE:

Though Francon is a more refined version of Keating, they are similar because they both share the same *modius operandi*: a method of operation characterized by convincing rich clients, with uninformed esthetic sensibilities, to hire them since everyone who is anyone agrees they are good designers and therefore deserve to be at the top of their profession. Despite this consensus, however, they are not good designers at all because they do not create original buildings of high structural, esthetic, and creative worth. Rather, they become famous architects because they know how to convince wealthy people that their buildings are elegant and graceful. A technique they complement with gourmet food and fine wines at the best restaurants. Said differently, Francon and Keating are similar because both men sooth people into becoming their clients by convincing prospective customers that their buildings are fashionable examples of the high style, since important people, like New York's intellectual elite, want their buildings. Further, both men ply their clients with esthetic rhetoric to accept their designs. But whereas Guy Francon is a truly gracious gentleman from the old classical school with highly refined interpersonal social skills – signaled by his elaborately civilized manners with other people – Peter Keating is not so gracious and not such a gentlemen. Though he pretends to be. Both, however, are mediocre architects who assign the hard design and structural work to others: Claude Stengel in Francon's case and Howard Roark in Keating's case.

What further distinguishes Francon from Keating is that Francon wins over clients and keeps finding new ones through: his network of Aristocratic contacts spawned by Lucius Heyer; his initial design work such as the Frink Bank Building (however inept); his tapping into Claude Stengel's competent design and able drafting skills; all supplemented by Keating's plagiarism of Roark's buildings. Keating, on the other hand, does not have the ability to pull such a fraud off. For he does not find an aristocratic partner as well connected as Lucius Heyer. Nor can he shunt the hard design work to a competent architect, like Claude Stengel. Nor is he lucky enough to find a protege like himself who conveys to him the competency of someone like a Howard Roark. This is why Keating's architectural firm *would* have failed immediately after opening—had he not spent his own money to keep it open—by imploding from its own incompetency.

In the final analysis, Guy Francon and Peter Keating would have been happier if they followed their real values from a more modest life-station instead of elevating themselves into unmerited positions they do not deserve.

(39) ANALYSIS OF THE DIFFERENCE BETWEEN ROARK & THE REVELERS:

The difference between Roark and the revelers is that Roark loves his career, loves his job, enjoys creative work, and relishes being a great architect, while the revelers hate their careers, hate their jobs, spurn creative work, and lack a focus in life. It seems the revelers *merely* withstand the boring motions of a draining profession by repeating the dull routines of a vapid job. Instead of choosing meaningful careers like Roark does—which is evident by the ecstasy he experiences when he builds the Heller house—the revelers *merely* tolerate their jobs as a necessary burden to be endured, executing their employment responsibilities with a minimum of effort while looking forward to a maximum of vacation. Evidently, their life's goal is to escape the monotonous routine of a stultifying job by interspersing their work with copious amounts of leisure, only tolerating their jobs for a paycheck. So they can buy the necessities of life (i.e. water, food, clothing, and shelter) so they do not freeze to death in the winter, boil to death in the summer, starve from malnutrition, or parch from dehydration. So they can exist. Not live. So they can give to their bodies what their bodies naturally need to survive. Nothing less. Nothing more. All for a bit of money. For pecuniary remuneration that barely enables them to live a half-way decent life. Accordingly all the revelers contemplate at work is somehow getting through the day, enduring the week, and surviving the month, so they can pay their bills on time, looking forward to the day when they can vacation, when they can retire, when they do not have to work. In essence, the revelers perfunctorily cling to their jobs with a sense of grim resignation, since they feel they must put food on the table in whatever way they can.

Conversely, if the revelers really loved their jobs. If they chose stimulating careers that personally meant something to them, they would enjoy working everyday, not *just* playing occasionally. But instead of working with eagerness the revelers look forward to knocking-off from work, so they can clack their uppers in sloppy bull sessions. So they can shriek to the sky in a howling hootenanny, since by yelling to the heavens they can evade for a time a series of deadening tasks connected to a job they should never have taken. Thus, the revelers goof-off on their off-days to escape the drudgery of their 9-5's. Accordingly they neither celebrate work milestones nor commemorate personal hallmarks by having a good time with special friends. Rather the revelers blow-off steam (i.e. they release their pent-up anxieties) by yelling their frustrations to the heavens. If they were passionate about their careers they would not be hedonistic pleasure seekers intent on leisure. Instead they would be ardent about their objectives. But the revelers do not work rewarding jobs that match their inner souls with their outer actions. They only endure the unpleasantries of their exasperating jobs for money, while looking forward to frolicking in the countryside to evade work. For jaunty pastoral frippery is the revelers only release from the vexations of their wearisome lives.

In the final analysis, the revelers are extremely dissatisfied with their work lives since their day jobs do not express who they are as people. And because the revelers never synergize who they are as people with their careers they do not know what they want, why they want it, nor how to get it. In other words, since the revelers do not connect their work lives to their identities they have no incentive to perform well on the job. Rather, they function like mindless drones who thoughtlessly repeat a set of perfunctory tasks at work like a military task master, instead of challenging themselves by learning new skills. Accordingly, they ramble through life in a desultory, diffused manner, lacking a coherent plan, a central purpose, and an intense passion for life. As such, the revelers lead blank lives empty of joy, optimism, and enthusiasm, since they have betrayed the best within them by doing what was expected of them. Not what they wanted or needed to do. The consolation prize for abandoning their souls is the reckless abandon they feel when they escape work. In brief, because the revelers never synchronize their inner beings to their outer actions, they are extremely dissatisfied with their jobs.

Unlike Roark, the revelers did not have the courage to build their own lives (i.e. to make their own way) despite what their parents, friends, or relatives wanted them to do. Rather, they gave in to what others wanted for them instead of finding the courage to create their own drive. Since the revelers have no singular devotion in life as Roark does. No one-track passion, they go through life lackadaisically, empty of ambition, hope, and joy.

Instead of choosing their own passions, selecting their own careers, and working suitable jobs of their own making, the revelers extinguish their dreams for a better life; smother their ambitions for a rewarding career; undercut their ability to pursue and achieve happiness by living the life they have instead of enjoying a life they made. What distinguishes Roark from the revelers is that while Roark makes his life's purpose architecture the revelers really do not know what they want nor how to get it. Ergo, they never really define a central purpose for their lives. Rather they pursue a hodgepodge of different types of jobs to eke out a meagre living, leaving one type of job, then starting something else anew, somewhere else, only to hop to something entirely different, and so on and so forth. That, or like Keating, they chose careers they do not want, do not understand, and are not good at because they lack the courage to do what they really want to do with their lives. Instead of projecting a long term, logically consistent plan for their lives, like Roark does, the revelers live for momentary pleasures only: Evanescent promises of happiness that vanish like a mirage when they approach. In other words, in place of pursuing satisfying careers the revelers betray their souls— which they never really understood in the first place—by settling for either a sequence of jobs that means little to them or a career that does not define who they really are. Accordingly, the revelers become mediocre at a lot of things but expert in nothing. Ergo, they live their lives going through the motions of their mundane existence without joy, meaning, or purpose, one day being just like the next which was just like the last, interspersed with brief glints of relief, marked by carousing with other fallen souls.

Unlike the revelers, Roark did not decide late in life (or not at all) what his purpose was. He did not hop from job-to-job in different fields. Nor did he choose a field he loathed. Rather, he knew he wanted to be an architect at age 12. Then he pursued that goal persistently and indefatigably, despite being hindered by many challenges along the way. Still he never gave up. He never gave in. He never decided to pursue a different line-of-work despite these setbacks. Unlike the revelers, Roark formed his life-plan when he was a child, when he was a teenager. Then he took steady actions to become an architect. This is why he enrolled at the Stanton Institute of Technology where he learned about structural engineering. This is why he worked summers as a plumber, plasterer, electrician, rivet catcher, and welder, to gain the practical experience he needed to understand how to build. When not studying or working he designed buildings, drafted blueprints, and built an architectural portfolio that he used to launch his career. Instead of oversocializing on his off-time Roark sketched buildings on his down time. After college he worked for Henry Cameron, the father of the modern skyscraper, thereby learning how to build. Before even attempting to construct his first major building Roark spent tens-of-thousands of hours working in trades related to architecture not only because he loved working with his hands but also so he could understand how to create good buildings. This is how Roark shows reader's that a person should find their purpose early in life (the earlier the better) develop a keen understanding of the discipline they are passionate about—through formal education, or self-teaching, or practical experience, or a combination thereof—while simultaneously developing the practical skills they need to flourish in their chosen career, through a series of pragmatic jobs in that field. Then, they should identify who the person is that can teach them what they want to know. And try to work with that person. If they qualify to be his, or her, understudy.

Sure, Roark underwent great difficulties along the way. And some of his life was routine. But he loved the routine because it connected to who he is as a person. Accordingly, the repetition was worth it to him because by repeatedly drafting buildings Roark inculcated the design skills he needed to be a great architect. Eventually, Roark's repetitive drafting work put him in a position to build skyscrapers, like the Enright House, for example, or the Cord building, for instance, thereby paving the way to his ultimate success.

True, life, any life, even Roark's life, is characterized by some monotony and tedious spells. But because Roark built a career for himself that connected to who he is as a person, he is profoundly happy, even though for years he struggles just like the revelers do. Said differently, because Roark lives life on his own terms by building buildings his own way he is not only spiritually fulfilled but he stays the course despite what life throws at him. Because he built his own life. Conversely, the revelers reap the inevitable consequences of their foolish actions, which is detestation of their jobs, a desire to evade the office, coupled with the evanescent relief of boisterous lollygagging with confederates.

(40) ANALYSIS OF HOW ROARK ENTHUSES HIS EMPLOYEES:

Roark creates a special feeling of pride in the minds-and-hearts of his fellow creators, since he designs projects that enable his friends to showcase their abilities: be it in drafting; design; sculpting; or construction.

For instance, Mallory is able to sculpt how he wants to sculpt because of Roark. Donnigan is able to build how he wants to build because of Roark. Roark's draftsmen are able to draft how they want to draft because of Roark.

Because Roark employs his friends on a series of great projects—design jobs that channel the best within them—his coworkers love him since he enables them to shine. This is why Roark's workers follow him to the ends of the earth. To all his construction projects, whether it is a small housing commission, or a large summer resort. Because Roark enables his friends to be true to themselves.

This is why they miss him when he sails with Wynand. This is why they will forever remember the buildings they create with him. This is why they are happy working with Roark. This is why they love Roark.

In sum, because Roark enthuses his staffers, sculptors, and construction managers with his architectural vision, Roark's friends are happy to work with him.

(41) ANALYSIS OF WHY ARCHITECTS DISLIKE ROARK:

Many architects dislike Roark because he focuses only on building the best buildings he can design; not social networking, or subscribing to their various building philosophies.

To explain, Roark's singular focus on building great buildings – not on developing smooth emotional relationships with other people – rankles many architects (especially Peter Keating) since it calls into question their method of gaining prominence by social climbing instead of producing substantive work. In other words, instead of developing amiable personal relationships with every person he meets a la Peter Keating, Roark only cares about building great buildings, not about other people, which, in turn, militates the profession against him.

Indeed Roark is hated by many architects for refusing to embrace their manifold building philosophies, like Gordon L. Prescott, for example, with his nihilistic architectural philosophy, or Gus Webb, for instance, with his post modernistic view of building. Another architect named John Erik Snyte dislikes Roark because he does not adhere to his mongrel building style, which combines elements of Classicism, Gothic, Renaissance, Miscellaneous, and Modernism, into a new grotesque construction style. On the contrary, since Roark is a modernist builder with his own uncompromising vision, he does not allow Snyte to distort his work. Accordingly, he rips apart Synte's drawing of the *Heller House*, which makes Synte hate him even more. To the extent that he calls Roark an incompetent – client-stealing – chiseler at the Stoddard Trial.

Similarly, other architects, like Ralston Holcombe, for example, or Guy Francon, for instance, dislike Roark because he does not subscribe to their classical, or Renaissance, architectural philosophies. For Roark not only disobeys Francon's order to build the *Ferrell* building in a semi-classical design style – instead of the Dana Building-esque modernist vision the client wants – but he also refuses to join the Renaissance inspired Architects Guild of America, which Holcombe is president of. Evidently, because Roark refuses to adulterate his designs by fusing them with Francon's classical vision, or Holcombe's Renaissance vision, Guy Francon fires him from Francon & Hyer, while Ralston Holcombe sanctions his A.G.A. Bulletin mockery.

In sum, because many architects think that Roark will neither pay lip service to their types of buildings—nor compromise with their way of building—he becomes a *persona non grata*, or *bête noire*, to the profession. A dangerous figure who is not to be encouraged, since he goes against accepted architectural esthetics.

(42) ANALYSIS OF WHY THE PUBLIC DISLIKES ROARK:

The man on the street does not like Roark because his face is hard: not soft, gooey, and pliable, like many people's faces are. To elaborate, something in Roark's *visage* tells the average man that he does not want to meet them, talk to them, or collaborate with them, since he does not care about them. And they are right to think that Roark does not care about them since he says: "'Can you see the campus and the town? Do you see how many men are walking and living down there? Well, I don't give a damn what any or all of them think about architecture—or about anything else, for that matter" (11). In brief, because people sense that Roark does not want to be friends with them they hate him for it, since he will do his own thing regardless of them.

In conclusion, though Roark is hated by large segments of the general public, largely ignored by other architects, and is kept poor for a significant part of the book, he never compromises his artistic principles for social acceptance.

(43) ANALYSIS OF HOW ROARK ONLY VALUES CAMERON'S ARCHITECTURAL JUDGMENT:

Roark only cares about what able architects, such as Henry Cameron, think about his work, since Cameron is the novel's only builder who can judge Roark's work accurately. Other than Cameron's evaluations, Roark ignores what anybody else thinks of his buildings, because he has better esthetic judgment than all of them combined: despite their supposed authority, or what buildings they have designed, or what they think constitutes a good structure.

(44) ANALYSIS OF HOW WORKING IN A ROCK QUARRY IS THERAPEUTIC FOR ROARK:

Since architecture is Roark's *sine qua non* he does whatever it takes to stay in the building trades, since he is only whole with architecture in his life. Conversely, without architecture he is incomplete. He is imperfect. He is not a full man. He is lesser. Therefore, he will not abandon architecture despite what the world throws at him, since architecture is what Roark has trained his mind, body, and spirit for his entire life: from age 10 to age 26. Indeed, since architecture deeply connects to who Roark is as a person he will do what he must do to be a successful builder, come hell-or-high water, which includes – but is not limited to – toiling in a blazing quarry inferno. In a way, Roark even likes working in the rock quarry, since grueling physical labor enables him to push his mind-and-body to the limit, so he can blast away any trace of self-pity before it crops-up, thereby permitting him to preserve who he is as a person by taking actions consistent with his identity. By focusing on chiseling rock, not mulling over ideas about how unfair the world is to him, Roark earns survival money. So he can resume his career as a *sui generis* architect. Gladly, Roark is saved from rock quarry work by Roger Enright, an independent businessman who summons him to New York to offer him a job designing an apartment building called Enright Homes.

Indeed, by calling Roark to Manhattan, Enright shows readers that Roark follows his own path, despite great hardships, by resuming building buildings his own way, since a client has seen and likes his buildings and thus wants to hire him.

(45) ANALYSIS OF ROARK'S CORTLANDT SPEECH:

First, Roark catalogues the basic creations of early men—*such as the wheel, for example, which permitted people to travel farther distances with less effort thereby easing commerce* – or *fire, for instance, which enabled people to cook and sanitize their food, stay warm, and increase their life spans.* Next, Roark says that instead of being rewarded (or at least thanked) for harnessing fire, or inventing the wheel, creators of these two improvements where likely burned on a stake – or torn to shreds on a rack – for daring to create something that made everyone's life better. Evidently, Roark analogizes his hounding by *so-called* civilization to the brutality his creative predecessors faced during the dark ages to define his persecution for what it is not what people think (or pretend) it is.

Second, Roark references how Adam was expelled from the *Garden of Eden* for eating an apple from the tree of knowledge to show readers that according to Christianity a drive to learn constituted a grave and unforgivable original sin that caused a person to be cast out of paradise into a harsh and unforgiving general world. Here, Roark questions the two-thousand-year-old Christian tradition of relying on faith to answer life's basic questions, since he relies on facts and evidence and logical reasoning to draw conclusions, not blind devotion.

Third, Roark says that legendary men who stood alone and thought for themselves, like Adam from the Bible, for example, or Prometheus from Greek pagan-mythology, for instance, paid for their bravery with unspeakable acts of cruelty. That visionaries, such as the Wright brothers, who invented the airplane, or pioneers, such as Edmund Cartwright, who invented the power loom, or creators, such as Thomas Davenport, who invented the motor, instead of being honored by humanity, were hated by many people. Roark continues that path-breaking astronomers, such as Galileo, who observed that the earth revolves around the sun, or serious thinkers, such as Servetus, who made important contributions to anatomy and medicine, or revolutionary scientists, like Einstein, who discovered the law of general relativity, were either denounced by their peers, heckled by the masses, or met with stern opposition until they either triumphed, like Einstein did, or were stagnated by ignorance, like Galileo was, or were burned alive by zealots, like Michael Servetus [3] was.

Third, Roark says that historically the motive of great creators was never to help, or serve, or enlighten his fellow man, but to pursue and achieve truth, his own truth, in his own way. Accordingly, the creator's purpose to Roark is to engender a unique creation of some sort. Then to enjoy that creation long after creating it. Because to Roark the process of creation to a creator presupposes that the creator holds his truth above all things and all men.

Fourth, Roark links creation to thinking for yourself, feeling for yourself, and judging for yourself. Since, to Roark there is no such thing as a collective thought, a collective brain, or a collective stomach: such as

---

[3] Michael Servetus: had wide ranging interests in science, medicine, theology, law, and the humanities. He made important contributions in medicine and anatomy: he was the first European to correctly describe blood circulation between the heart and lungs, independently of Ibn al-Nafis in Egypt. He was pronounced a heretic by Protestant and Catholic Churches, because he denied the Trinity and he objected to the baptism of infants. He was burned at the stake in Geneva, Switzerland. Any books Servetus had authored that could be found by religious authorities were also burned, so the importance of his work was unknown until many years after his death.

the assimilative world of the *Borg* on *Star Trek*. Rather, Roark believes that every original thought comes from the mind of one man, who functions – to the best of his ability – as a "fount of energy, a life force, a prime mover," who serves nothing and no one (711). And, thus, only lives for his work and only works for his life. Further, Roark infers that while other people can respect, love, and emulate other great people—just like Roark learns from Henry Cameron—ultimately a protege should not unthinkingly repeat what another person says, no matter who that person is, what authority they supposedly have, or what they think they know. Rather, Roark suggests that a person should create his own vision (not copy someone else's) since every human being has his own mind which cannot be shared. That, in sum, if a man frees his mind from other people's minds to think for himself, he can achieve great accomplishments that will not only benefit himself, personally, first-and-foremost, but that will advance humanity as well. As a secondary byproduct.

Fifth, Roark tells us that the human-mind is an individual's tool of survival since it enables a person to: build weapons to hunt for food; fashion tools to harvest crops; construct a home to keep the elements out; and sanitize water to survive. That while wild animals depend on claws, fangs, horns, strong muscles, and instincts to survive, human beings rely on their minds to flourish. Accordingly Roark tells readers that human beings use their minds to figure out natural laws, adapt their environments to them, and create inventions to improve their lives. As opposed to animals that rely on automatic instincts evolved over millennia to sense resources and travel to abundance. Accordingly, Roark suggests that since humans beings are reasonable-rational-creatures—not instinct-based wild animals—everything humans do to survive requires a process of thought, not a reliance on automatic cyclical patterns of behavior.

Sixth, Roark contrasts the original thinker, the primary creator, or the principal producer, who flourishes in life by using reason, with the second-hander, the second-rater, the mooching parasite, who seeks to attach himself to a producer so he can siphon-off benefits from that producer, since the parasite does not want to work to earn material values. He would rather exercise effort for the sake of non-effort. For the second hander lives not by creating something, however modest, according to his skill level. He exists by taking away other people's work-product by bullying his way into the first-handers life, since he needs producers to survive. In this regard, Roark suggests that while a primary creator, like him, focuses on work, focuses on nature, and focuses on building, a spiritual parasite, like Toohey, spends all his life destroying values, destroying creators, taking control of men's minds, moving them into positions of influence, so he can consolidate his own power by forming a legion of buffers, who act as intermediaries between him and a natural reality that he is helpless to understand or survive in. Further, Roark infers that arch second-handers like Toohey depend on people to exist, while he, the arch first hander, only needs himself to flourish. In sum, whereas the primary creator does not care about the opinions of *most* others—except for people he chooses to work with—for the parasite others are his prime motive.

Seventh, Roark suggests that while "the basic need of a creator is [intellectual] independence," emotional self-sufficiency, and physical self-reliance, "the basic need of the second-hander is to secure ties with [other] men to be fed" since parasites could not survive if it were not for a set of creators to produce for them. So they can piggy-back off their inventions. (712). But first-handers, Roark infers, do not need other people to live-off of because they are wholly self-sufficient.

Eighth, Roark suggests that a reasoning mind cannot work under any form of compulsion whatsoever—either from the dictatorship of the masses, who form social pressure groups that tell creators what to do; or from a tyrannical boss, who orders a creator around like a slave instead of treating said creator fairly, or from an assemblage of so-called peers who heap enormous amounts of pressure on a person because they want to take over or eradicate their vision.

(46) ANALYSIS OF HOW KEATING TRIES TO MAKE ROARK LIKE HIM & WHY:

Keating tries to convince Roark to be a social metaphysician like he is (i.e. a person who manipulates others to succeed) so he can prove to himself that the only way to achieve in life is by coaxing others.

Thus, Keating tells Roark that if he becomes a *gamesmen* architect like he is he will make copious amounts of money, achieve great fame, and win deserved recognition. That to succeed in life one must play and win this sort of social game. Otherwise, he will be alienated, mocked, and stomped on, until he is caused to fail.

Keating says this because he must make Roark like him. He must make Roark into a person who *also* games his clients, bamboozles his bosses, and creates superficial friendships over fine wines and elegant dinners.

Indeed, to feel better about himself Keating must: undermine Roark's design principles; water down Roark's drafting values; and get Roark to manipulate others like he does, so that Roark becomes like him. One of the good old boys who tricks the public into thinking he is an exceptional architect when he is not. In brief, Keating must bring a man like Roark down to his own average architectural level, so he can preserve his own *modus operandi*. So he does not have to question the morality of what he does. So he does have to cast doubt on his method of getting ahead in life without really trying.

Thus, Keating's fear in this scene, which he masks with a thin veneer of fake benevolence, underscores the idea that he needs to comfort himself into believing that he was right to rise through gamesmanship all along, since it is impossible to rise by substantive content alone like Howard Roark does.

(47) ANALYSIS OF HOW ROARK'S PHILOSOPHY OF RATIONAL EGOISM LEADS TO SUCCESS WHILE KEATING'S PHILOSOPHY OF ALTRUISTIC SACRIFICE LEADS TO FAILURE:

The Fountainhead shows readers that rising by altruism ultimately leads to suffering and failure, while a properly selfish philosophy (i.e. objectivism) leads to joy and success. The novel does this by contrasting Howard Roark's eventual triumph to Peter Keating's ultimate failure.

To be clear while Roark's philosophy of rational egoism enables him to: live life his own way; earn merited pay; gain deserved public recognition; and win the woman he loves, Keating's philosophy of altruism leads to him sacrificing his values for prestige; abandoning his soul to gain influence; losing the woman he loves; and being recognized as a fraud. For Keating's altruistic life-sensations leads to critical failure on an intellectual, moral, and spiritual level – since he ends-up careerless, loveless, and hopeless since he embraced self-sacrifice – while Roark's Objectivism leads to him rising to success as an architect, a lover, and a human being. Said differently, because Keating sacrifices others to himself by expending people he thinks are in his way – such as Tim Davis, for example, or Claude Stengel, for instance, or Lucius Hyer, case in point – his philosophy of sacrificing others to himself ultimately causes him to fail. Whereas Roark's non-sacrificial policy of building like-minded others up. (i.e. Steven Mallory and Mike Donnigan) helps him succeed, since he realizes his selfish values by trading with other competent individuals.

In short, Keating's final downfall not only shows readers that a human being who manipulates his way to the top eventually crashes down to the bottom, his tragic end illustrates how altruism and collectivism eventually leads to depression and failure while egoism and individualism eventually leads to happiness and success.

(48) ANALYSIS OF ROARK NOT TRYING TO OUTDO OTHERS LIKE KEATING BUT MEASURING HIS OWN WORTH BY HIS ARTISTIC INTEGRITY:

Unlike Keating, Roark does not compete with other architects by contemplating whether his buildings are better than theirs, or not. Rather, Roark builds as he sees fit, regardless of what other people think, say, or do. For Roark never thinks of himself in comparison to other people (i.e. how his work relates to theirs). Rather, Roark measures his own value by the inherent quality of his architectural designs, independent of how those architectural designs correlate to existing buildings. For he is not concerned with his superiority over others (i.e. whether he is smarter, or stronger, or better-looking than his fellow man). Rather, he only focuses on being the best architect he can be. Accordingly, all of Roark's mental energies are directed towards him developing the skills he needs to build the sort of buildings he needs to produce. Not on trying to outdo others.

(49) ANALYSIS OF HOW DONNIGAN AND ROARK ARE BOTH FIRST HANDERS:

Evidently, Donnigan uses his reasoning mind to ascertain that Roark is a first-hander, not a second-hander, since first-handers make up their own minds about people, situations, and events. Whereas second handers merely rely on others opinions to form their own positions, since what gets a second-hander to believe a thing is not necessarily what is so but what most people agree is so. Popular agreement, then, becomes the second-handers metric of evaluation. Conversely, first handers, like Mike Donnigan, use their own independent judgment to determine what an individual is, or is not, independent of what anyone else thinks.

(50) ANALYSIS OF HOW ROARK & DONNIGAN RECOGNIZE & APPRECIATE EACH OTHER'S COMPETENCE:

Because Donnigan first watches Roark melt a perfect hole in a metal beam, then sees him walk on a girder like the most seasoned construction worker, he thinks Roark is an able builder. Similarly, Roark thinks Mike is competent because he sees Donnigan diligently scaffolding buildings, installing piping, putting in electrical wires, plastering walls, and more, on several construction projects. In the final analysis, then, Roark and Donnigan become good friends, since they are both able builders who love their professions.

(51) ANALYSIS OF WHY ROARK & DONNIGAN ARE LIKE EACH OTHER:

Roark and Donnigan are alike because both men look for and revere competency of any sort, especially in building, since Mike "worships expertness of any kind" and Roark "respond[s] only to the essence of a man: to his creative capacity [because in his] office one [has] to be competent." (86, 317). They are also alike because they both do not "tolerate anything other [than] single-track devotions" (86). Further, they love each other because Roark admires how Donnigan builds while Donnigan venerates how Roark designs and builds. Because of this shared architectural love, then, they both become experts at acetylene torch welding, since they both need to learn how to build buildings better from the ground up. This is why they both love constructing buildings together on many different construction projects, such as the Heller House, for example, or Monadnock Valley, for instance, because both men know how to build.

Further, they both share similar identities, since they both seek out and work for the same grand master architect – i.e. Henry Cameron – since they both recognize, and thus want to learn from, his architectural genius, since Cameron is the absolute best at what he does. And they know it.

Roark also likes Donnigan because Donnigan uses his mind to determine what is or is not the case, just like he does. For Donnigan and Roark both use their own cognition (i.e. evidence gathered through their five senses) to evaluate situations, people, and events, realistically. This is why when a building supervisor says that Roark is a "stuck-up, stubborn, lous[y] bastard"—Donnigan does not believe him, since this criticism contradicts what Donnigan has seen and heard from Roark (86).

In short, Roark is like Donnigan, and Donnigan is like Roark, because they are both career-driven men who love architecture and building respectively. Enough to become great at it.

(52) ANALYSIS OF WHY KEATING IS HAPPY THAT ROARK IS EXPELLED FROM STANTON:

Keating is happy that Roark is expelled from Stanton for four reasons. One, he is gladdened because Roark's expulsion convinces him that he is Stanton's top graduate – first in his class without peer – which he was never really sure of. Two, Keating delights in Roark's removal, since his ousting not only ostensibly rids him of a worthy Stanton opponent, who he now thinks is a flop, but he is especially happy since he now thinks that no reputable firm will hire someone who was booted from design school. Four, Keating takes heart at Roark's academic exclusion, since he now thinks that Roark cannot possibly challenge him down the road, as a professional architect, because noone will hire a man with an *alleged* critically tarnished record. Three, Keating is overjoyed that Roark is expelled from Stanton, since he now thinks – fully for the first time – that Roark's expulsion validates his method of rising in the field not because he is a visionary architect with superlative designing and drafting skills but because he knows how to game the system. Because he knows how to pull wool over people's eyes, by manipulating them into giving him: high grades; academic honors; and work promotions. Since he knows how to trick traditional ivory towered scholars, like Stanton's Dean, for example, or industry heavy hitters, like Guy Francon, for instance, to recognize and reward his way of fraudulent building, while dismissing and punishing Roark's *sui generis* method of design.

In sum, Roark's expulsion convinces Keating that his social climbing way of getting ahead in architecture without really trying—through communal networking not substantive style—is the only way he can succeed.

However, Keating learns, by novel's end, that an unforgiving reality proves otherwise.

(53) ANALYSIS OF KEATING'S GUILTY PLEASURE AT ROARK'S EXPULSION:

Keating experiences *schadenfreude* – or a guilty pleasure – when Roark is expelled from Stanton, since he knows he should not be happy at Roark's misfortune, since such an emotion is not an honorable sentiment to feel. But he feels happy anyway, even though he knows he should not, because he thinks his way of building is validated with Roark's removal. At least Keating has enough grace to feel a *guilty* sense of pleasure at Roark's expulsion, since he recognizes, on some level, that Roark should be honored and cherished for his work. Not expelled.

(54) ANALYSIS OF KEATING'S GRADUATION SPEECH:

During his graduation speech, Keating proudly holds his head high, boldly pronounces clichés about the glory of building, deftly strikes a tone of courtesy deference, all to convince the gray-hairs present to hire him. Because he is like them. One of the good old boys who can help them draft, design, and produce the kind of buildings that they want, since they think that a pupil who graduated first in his Stanton class must be a good architect. For Stanton is *the most* prestigious architectural school in the country. Even though *it is not* the best one.

Ergo, Keating convinces them, with his humble body posture, submissive non-verbal cues, and beseeching looks, that he is an able protégé who will defer to their more senior wisdom. Sadly, however, they fail to realize that he only appears to be modest, honest and natural, when he is not humble, forthright, or authentic. They also do not understand that his fake abilities, fake humility, and fake love for others, are all ploys to disguise his lack of mastery. For senior designers do not realize that Keating imitates a desire to learn, not because he loves architecture and thus needs to learn about it. But because he wants to manipulate his way to the top by wheedling other people.

Ergo, Keating's direct eye contact, assertive voice, and proud bearing, projects false confidence – to the assembled host – not real self-assurance. For Keating is so good at role playing that senior architects do not realize he is a patent phony (i.e. a smooth operator who affects an unreal pose).

Keating affects this unreal pose because he realizes that senior architects do not want to work with a cocky braggart, one the one hand, who will not take their counsel. Nor a diffident milksop, on the other hand, who is too afraid to assert himself because he lacks self-confidence. Rather Keating understands that they want to work with a modest person who balances his inner confidence, on the one hand, gained from his hard-won abilities, with workplace guidance, on the other hand, that they will provide. Keating realizes this. Thus, he pretends to be willing to learn from them, via a properly "humble" attitude towards his work. So that his audience thinks he is basically a capable learner draftsman (i.e. an able entry-level prospect) who will not overstep his architectural bounds by faking skills he does not have.

Thus, to hide his architectural mediocrity, Keating utters bromides such as "Truth, Love and Beauty" (19). Which sound good, on the face of it, the problem is that Keating does not care for truth, does not love his fellow man, and has not accomplished beauty. If he sought the truth he would not have pretended that Roark's work was his own. If he loved his fellow-man he would not have cast out his brothers, such as Tim Davis, Claude Stengel, and Lucius Hyer. If he valued beauty, and had the skill to produce it, he would not have designed ugly buildings, such as Lois Cook's horrid bowery residence. But, it is okay, since Keating embraces Stanton's esthetic design philosophy by telling his professors what they want to hear:

that "architecture is a great art, [therefore] architects should look to the future" with their minds but respect the past with their hearts, since architecture is a "sociological craft" (19).

Despite projecting confidence with a modulated voice, good eye contact, and a dynamic delivery, internally, Keating is a mess. He is extremely frightened about delivering an architectural speech to an assembly of renowned architects, since he knows he is a mediocre builder (at best) who has no *real* right to address them, since Keating recognizes (on some level) that he is a fraud who does not really deserve the honors that Stanton gives him.

(55) ANALYSIS OF KEATING'S UNIVERSITY SUCCESS & ROARK'S UNIVERSITY FAILURE:

Unlike Roark, who knows a lot about architecture, Keating does not know how to design, despite cultivating some mediocre building skills. Therefore, he is an average architect, at best. But in gaining other people's favor he is a master, since he has won over both his professors and his peers with his charm.

He wins over his professors by adhering to conventional art traditions that they embrace by producing traditional esthetic assignments that they like: assignments that help them perpetuate established design precedents by meeting standard architectural expectations. Further, Keating's professors like him because he helps them manage other students, both in class and across campus, since he is their duly elected leader. Keating's professors also like him for helping them bring athletic monies to the University by heading the track-and-field team. Similarly, students like Keating because he tricks them into believing he is their good friend, by casting a warm glow on them with his kind eyes, which makes his peers feel all warm and fuzzy inside. Students also like him for voicing their concerns to the faculty senate, so that their voices are heard. They also like him for creating a festive party atmosphere as an extroverted fraternity member, so they can enjoy themselves socially, unrestrainedly.

Indeed, since Keating psychologically manipulates the students and faculty by being what they want him to be, they decide to make him "president of the student body, captain of the track team, [and] member of the most important fraternity, [thereby granting him the title of] the most popular man on campus" (17).

Though Keating is smooth on the outside—characterized by the genial radiance of his cordial eyes—he is lamentable on the inside. Not only because he pretends to be competent and benevolent when he is not. But, most importantly, because he has not learned the one thing he went to Stanton to learn. Namely, to build. To design quality buildings that are new and creative; not structures that simply rehash past building traditions.

What makes Keating's lack of originality even worse, however, is that he deceives his professors, much of the time, by relying on Roark's genius to fix his confusions, instead of rising, or falling, by his own merits or demerits. Accordingly, Keating is an average architect, at best, or a fraudulent pretender, at worst, because he cannot *even* give his professors what they want without Roark's help.

Roark, on the other hand, is not the head of the student body; the captain of the track team; nor the president of a fraternity. Nor was he voted the most popular man on campus. But he is a great architect, which should be, but sadly is not, the most important quality of a Stanton Graduate. Since Roark does not conform to his professor's second-rate method of architecture, he is hated by most of the faculty. Such as his professor of design, professor Peterkin, for example, who threatens to resign if he is not expelled. Further, he is not appreciated by many of his other professors, since he presents a *sui generis* building vision of his own, contrary to what they teach.

Yet the scorn Roark receives from *most* of his professors is understandable (though not excusable) since he violates everything they have been taught to admire and value in architecture. Indeed, since Roark's buildings are too radical for them, his professors malign his structures most of the time.

In sum, Stanton professors disparage Roark and value Keating not only because Keating knows how to speak the faculties language by devising buildings that they expect and like – while Roark does not – but also because they fail to understand that Roark is the real mind behind any decent buildings that Keating designed.

In sum, the difference between Keating and Roark, is that while Roark actually loves his work, loves to be challenged by architectural problems, and designs unassigned projects on his off-time, Keating does not love architecture, does not love his work and is only willing to do what is required of him at school for the prestige he can gain from architecture.

(56) ANALYSIS OF HOW KEATING LOOKS FOR OTHERS FLAWS TO MAKE HIMSELF FEEL BETTER:

Keating must out-do everyone. He must one-up them, to make himself feel better than others, because he values himself not based on how good he is in the absolute sense, independent of anyone else. But in relation to how good he is when compared to other people. Thus, when Keating needs cheering-up, he notes how handsome he is in relation to his unattractive coworkers, since this comparison is self-gratifying, since it imbues Keating with warm feelings of superiority for being better than ugly people.

(57) ANALYSIS OF KEATING'S HONESTY WITH ROARK:

Keating is honest with Roark when they are alone. When it is just them two talking. Because when they are in *mono-et-mono* conversations, Keating tells Roark what is really on his mind and in his heart instead of performing. Instead of faking reality by voicing others beliefs. For when alone with Roark, Keating does not express safe thoughts he thinks other people want to hear. Rather, he articulates what he truly believes, without the pressure to pretend. Without the compulsion to conform.

In sum, during their private conversations Keating opens up to Roark; is genuine with Roark; shows Roark who he really is, by telling Roark what he really thinks, feels, and believes, as he does with no other person, except Catherine Halsey.

(58) ANALYSIS OF HOW KEATING COULD HAVE CHOSEN A BETTER PATH:

By the end of the story, we learn that Keating would have been happier if his ruling purpose in life was first-handed creation characterized by his own value-oriented reason for being, not engaging in architectural fraud to extract money from society. Or manipulating people to gain respect in other people's eyes but not his own. Or attaining an elevated social station that he does not deserve.

But he does not have the courage to do all these things. Instead he sacrifices his values by selling his soul to Toohey, thereby reaping the inexorable consequences of his foolish actions, which is complete psychological ruination; no romantic love life to speak of; and widespread hatred from his fellow man for defrauding the general public.

Indeed, Keating would have been more fulfilled if he became a good artist rather than a fraudulent architect. If he married a woman he loved (Catherine Halsey) instead of a woman people would ogle over (Dominique Francon). If he was guided by his own internal moral compass instead of being directed by the opinions of others.

(59) ANALYSIS OF KEATING'S DISSOLUTION:

Tragically, Keating's career is ruined after the Cortlandt trial, his body is fattened from over eating and over-drinking. He goes to a cabin somewhere, to doodle art works that any child could paint. And his remaining days, if he has enough money to live on, are characterized by barricading himself in his room, filling out crossword puzzles, and splotching paint on a canvas. Utterly depressed, Keating realizes – with his last bit of mental coherence – that he could have been a good artist. Yet he betrayed himself (i.e. the best within him) for fame and prestige, instead of building his own life.

(60) ANALYSIS OF KEATING'S ARCHITECTURAL PHILOSOPHY:

Keating thinks that to be a successful architect all he needs to know are four things. One, how to convince people that he is a good architect when he is not. Two, how to win people over by flattering their sensibilities. Three, how to persuade people to back him by winning their affections. And, four, how to remove people blocking his rise. And if he is stumped during his career, no sweat, he can get people, like Roark, who have greater skills than he does, to produce substantive work that he can take credit for.

(61) ANALYSIS OF HOW KEATING RELIES ON ROARK TO TRANSFER HIS SCHOOL SUCCESS TO THE OFFICE:

Because Keating thinks that social climbing yielded fruit in school he continues to manipulate people at work, since he feels that what worked at one place will surely work in another. This is why he continues to tap the mind of his genius friend Howard Roark to succeed, since without his help he could not have made the grade in school, gotten a job with Francon & Hyer, nor designed his two best buildings. And though the Keating technique does gain him some short-term fraudulent success in other people's eyes, once people discover that Roark designed all of Keating's best buildings (i.e. the Cosmo-Slotnick Building, for example, or the Cortlandt Building, for instance) his reputation is ruined and his career over, for people realize that Keating never designed the buildings he takes credit for.

(62) ANALYSIS OF THE EFFECTS OF PETER KEATING'S FRAUD:

In the final analysis, Keating is exposed as a sham, during the Cortlandt trial, when he divulges that he did not design Cortlandt, but instead took credit for another man's work. This confession not only dissolves his reputation in the minds of others but it also dissolves his sense of honor in his own eyes.

(63) ANALYSIS OF WHY KEATING DOES NOT FOLLOW ROARK'S ADVICE EVEN THOUGH HE RESPECTS ROARK'S JUDGEMENT:

Though Keating follows the Dean's advice, Guy Francon's advice, and Toohey's advice, he respects Roark's advice above the counsel of all others, since Roark's guidance is realistic. But since Keating wants to social-climb his way to the commanding heights of the architectural profession, he follows the recommendations of traditional academics, classical architects, and Marxist socialists, since he is a gamesman who manipulates people to succeed.

(64) ANALYSIS OF KEATING'S FALL AND ROARK'S SUCCESS:

Though Keating is not an evil character, he is an infinitely pathetic one, whom readers feel sorry for, since he becomes a broken-down wretch by the end of the novel, while Roark, who everyone thought would fail, actually rises to the pinnacle of the profession, by matching his unique architectural vision with masterful design skills. And though Roark is not after prestige, authority, or riches, he gets these accolades by being true to himself.

(65) ANALYSIS OF HOW THE KEATING'S MAKE MONEY:

Besides rental income and her deceased husband's life-insurance annuity, Peter Keating supplements the Keating's family income by clerking in hotels and posing for hat commercials.

(66) ANALYSIS OF KEATING ABANDONING HIS CHILDHOOD DREAM TO BE AN ARTIST:

Evidently, Peter's mother rejects her son's desire to be an artist, since she wants Peter to be a prestigious architect who lives in an expensive apartment in Manhattan not a ragged artist with ripped jeans living in a dilapidated art studio in Soho. Perhaps, if Mrs. Keating let her son follow his own passion, he would have become a great artist. But because Mrs. Keating imposes her own idea of success on Peter, she ultimately crushes his dreams before he has a chance to shine, since she wants him to be respected in other people's eyes, never mind what he thinks of himself. Thus, part of the reason why Mrs. Keating pushes Peter into a career he never wanted and did not choose is because she wants to feel vicariously successful through him. However, because Peter follows his mother's dreams instead of his own he becomes a mediocre architect (at best) who designs average buildings. He even resorts to fraud when he expropriates Roark's designs, since he does not have the mind (nor the will) to design masterful buildings himself. Ultimately, since Keating follows his mother's advice (not his own inner voice) he feels empty inside. And though by novel's end he tries to reconnect to his passion for painting by designing canvasses in an isolated cabin in the woods, at 50 it is too late for him to become a good visual artist since his youth's substantial energies are already spent.

(67) ANALYSIS OF KEATING BEING INTERRUPTED BY HIS MOTHER:

When Keating is in a very honest conversation with Roark about whether he should go to the Ecole des Beaux Arts in Paris or whether he should work for Guy Francon in New York the two men are interrupted by his mother, who asks Keating and Roark to drink hot chocolate and eat cookies that she has prepared for them. In response to her sudden entrance Keating says "But, Mother, I wanted to speak to Howard about something important" (22). Nevertheless, Keating obediently rises to his feet and follows his mother into the kitchen, while Roark "shrugs, rises," and goes to the kitchen as well (22). Evidently, Mrs. Keating's unexpected interjection ruins the authentic moment between Peter and Roark, since with her present Peter is no longer 100 % honest with Roark as he was before. Instead, with her there, Keating resumes a flippant tone about going to the Ecole des Beaux Arts in Paris or working for Guy Francon in New York. Without being asked a thing, Mrs. Keating chimes in, "Now, Petey, let me get this straight..." (23). But before she finishes her sentence she is silenced by Peter, who says "Oh, wait a minute, Mother!... Howard, I've got to weigh it carefully. It isn't everyone who can get a scholarship like that." (23). Evidently, Peter tries to halt the conversation with his mother because he knows that once she voices her opinion he will follow her counsel regardless of what he wants. Therefore, with his mother present, Peter no longer entertains the idea (however faintly) of doing something else. Instead he boasts that he has to decide between two prestigious options: either going to the Ecole des Beaux Arts in Paris or working with Guy Francon in New York. In response, Keating's mother guilt trips her son into soliciting her opinion by saying: "You're quite right, Peter...On a question like that you don't want to consult your mother. It's too important. I'll leave you to settle it with Mr. Roark." (23). Evidently, Mrs. Keating knows her son. She knows that she can get invited to voice her opinion by pretending to be ready to leave. Her plan works because even though Peter "...did not want to hear what she thought [because he knows that] his only chance to decide [for himself is] to make the decision before he heard her" he allows her to speak nonetheless (23).

Evidently, Mrs. Keating uses pathos to appeal to Peter's sense of filial duty, since she "...looks at him [beseechingly] ready to turn and leave the room..." (23). Further, she manipulates Peter by appealing to his sense of wanting to outdo his classmates. This is why she says that if Peter does not work for Guy Francon, Ted Shlinker – his top Stanton competitor – will get the spot. Since Peter cannot brook the idea of anyone else outdoing him he decides to work for Francon & Hyer.

Again his mother wins the day, just like she did when he was a child, by persuading him to betray his inner voice. Perhaps, if Louisa Keating was not there at all, Peter would have realized, by talking to Roark, that he should drop everything and paint. But Keating does not make this epiphany because his mother summarily ends any authenticity between Peter and Roark with her presence.

(68) ANALYSIS OF WHY KEATING JILTS CATHERINE AND MARRIES DOMINIQUE:

Ironically, Dominique proposes marriage to Peter—just as he "...had been packing a suitcase..." to marry Catherine—not because she loves and wants to marry him but because Dominique wants to destroy her own capacity to admire greatness, so she is not hurt by the world (380). After little persuasion, then, Keating agrees to marry Dominique—even though he fears her—since he thinks a trophy wife like her will promote his career, while a clumsy wife, like Catherine, will retard his career. Even though Peter loves Catherine, feels comfortable with her, and Catherine loves him in return, he marries the boss's daughter anyway to impress others. Thus, "at nine o'clock [the next] morning Keating...pace[s] the floor of his room, his door locked...forget[ting] that it was nine o'clock and that Catherine was waiting for him [since he] makes himself forget her and everything she implied." (389). Here Keating sacrifices his next-day marriage to his true love Catherine Halsey to marry to an elegant woman he is actually scared of. This, then, is how he abandons his one remaining honest value in life (i.e. his simple love of a woman) for prestige.

In brief, Keating does not love Dominique and Dominique does not love Keating. Yet they marry anyway because Keating needs to be accompanied by an attractive lady that others will gape at while Dominique needs to eradicate her capacity for hero worship.

(69) ANALYSIS OF DOMINIQUE REFLECTING BACK TO KEATING WHO HE IS:

Part of Dominique's role in *The Fountainhead* is to reflect back to Keating who he is before it is too late: while he still has time to change.

Accordingly, Dominique copies Keating during their twenty-month marriage to show him that he has no self. That he has no soul. This is why she never thinks for herself, feels for herself, values for herself, makes important decisions for herself, defines a purpose for herself, wills a volition for herself, expresses a soul for herself, or develops an ego for herself during her marriage. Instead she becomes a mindless, soulless, lifeless, selfless, social-chameleon a la Peter Keating. A person who only is what others want her to be but is never herself in public, just like Peter Keating poses for others to manipulate them.

This is why Dominique always agrees with Keating – always does what he asks her to – always repeats trite bromides he sanctions over-and-over again, like the need to treat blue bloods with tolerance and respect, for example. Never once does she get angry at him; nor does she express her real opinion about anything — like what curtains she wants, for example, or what desert she would like to eat, for instance. Accordingly, she never suggests to Keating that they should do this or that. Not this or that. Instead she becomes a brainless body like Keating is – a person with no true-self.

Essentially, Dominique gives Keating what he wants by becoming what he is. Yet without the trimmings. Without disguising her inner emptiness with a thin veneer of false virtue. Accordingly, Dominique shapeshifts into what Keating is so Keating can see himself clearly, without the camouflage of an evasive ideology.

In sum, by dropping any pretense to virtue whatsoever Dominique hopes to get Keating to realize how empty he is inside, so that maybe, in time, he will develop an ego of his own, a will of his own, an independent spirit of his own, before it is too late. Before he totally wastes away.

(70) ANALYSIS OF HOW ROGER ENRIGHT RUNS HIS COMPANIES SINGLE HANDEDLY SINCE HE DOES NOT SELL SHARES OF HIS ENTERPRISES ON THE NEW YORK STOCK EXCHANGE:

Unlike many publicly traded companies that need permission from their executive board's for all major decisions, Roger Enright can hire

Roark to build Enright Homes on-the-spot without needing anybody's approval. Without having to cut through red tape. For Enright alone decides what projects his businesses undertake. This gives him incredible flexibility. Because without a board to hogtie him Enright can act solely on his own judgement.

(71) ANALYSIS OF HOW MALLORY IMMORTALIZES EXULTATION:

Steven Mallory immortalizes exultation in man by designing sculptures that emphasize the upward glance: such as the naked figure of Dominique Francon stretching her arms to the sky.

(72) ANALYSIS OF WHY WYNAND CORRUPTS PEOPLE WITH INTEGRITY:

Because Wynand needs to prove to himself that he had no choice but to betray his soul to make money and gain power, he corrupts individuals with firm principles, so he can convince himself that anyone can be corrupted. Even the most virtuous person. Thus, he keeps people like Dwight Carson around, regardless of cost, since he needs a carnal reminder, in the flesh-and-blood, that his own debasement was inevitable, since all men, any man, even the best man, will eventually fall from grace.

Ergo, to prove to himself that people must betray their beliefs (i.e. give up their values) to be successful, Wynand forces Dwight Carson to espouse the masses over the individual even though Carson believes the opposite. Indeed, by making Dwight Carson betray his values in this way, Wynand confirms to himself that people have no choice but to experience a split between what they believe deep-down – in the deep recesses of their inner essence – and what they do outwardly, to make money and gain power. Ultimately, Carson's self-betrayal confirms to Wynand that it is impossible to be both a moral man and a practical one. Such a perfect being – Wynand thinks – does not exist. It is only, at best, a pleasant fiction. Thus, when he corrupts people by getting them to betray their inner values, Wynand experiences fits of hysterical laughter—the purer the people he can corrupt the better.

(73) ANALYSIS OF HOW TOOHEY USES COLLECTIVIST IDEOLOGIES LIKE DIALECTICAL MATERIALISM AND SPIRITUAL MYSTICISM TO CONTROL PEOPLE EVEN THOUGH THESE PHILOSOPHIES ARE MORAL OPPOSITES:

Toohey uses many different collectivist philosophies to coax people into doing what he wants done. Like Dialectical materialism and spiritual mysticism, for example, which are antithetical opposites, since spiritual mysticism supports the idea of becoming one with the infinite and absolute spiritual energy of God, while dialectical materialism is a Marxist God denying philosophy of science and nature that states that religion is man-made, since any religion, all religions, is "the opiate of the masses." Toohey, it seems, will appeal to any popular thought system to bolster his own power, instead of consistently adhering to one principled stance.

(74) ANALYSIS OF HOW ABSTRACT BUSINESS THEORIES ARE UNIMPORTANT TO HOMER SLOTTERN:

To Homer Slottern the idea that the customer is always right, even when they are wrong, does not apply. To him what matters is that an item sells in his department store. Not its intrinsic qualities, such as its craftsmanship, or the manufacturing process behind it, or if it solves real-world problems, or if it is priced appropriately, or built to last. Consequently, the abstract theory behind a product does not really matter to Homer Slottern. What matters to him is that his customers buy what they think is good and what they think they want—even if they are disappointed with their purchase later—because ultimately, what's important to him, is how much short-term revenue he can squeeze out of his patrons, not the long-term reputational characteristics of his products. For this reason Homer Slottern even thinks that matching his business judgment with short-term customer fads is actually good for business, because such a policy may do him *most* well in the near-term, even if it tanks his department stores in the long term. In this connection, good business practices, such as lasting customer satisfaction (based on quality workmanship) and repeat business (based on appropriate pricing) seem irrelevant to Homer Slottern, since he values short-term practical trends over long-term business theories.

(75) ANALYSIS OF HOW DOMINIQUE TRIES TO SAVE ROARK FROM SUFFERING:

To spare Roark the inevitable pain of social rejection, Dominique wrests commissions away from him as a form of spiritual mercy killing.

(76) ANALYSIS OF HOW ROARK'S STODDARD HOME IS DISFIGURED BY JACKIE AND WEBB:

We see by this child's gobble-de-gook how the form and purpose of a building can be disfigured by another person. In this case a sub-normal child who debases the work of a master architect by grafting her amateurish self-expression onto it. This concept is most obvious when Webb distorts Roark's Cortlandt Homes by "building a cubistic ornament to frame the original windows, [then erecting] a modern neon sign on the roof, which read[s]: 'The Hopton Stoddard Home for Subnormal Children'" (397). In brief, Webb and Jackie's disfigurements of Roark's buildings demonstrate Roark's point that: "an honest building, like an honest man, [has] to be of one piece and one faith" (195).

(77) ANALYSIS OF JESSICA PRATT ADVOCATING FOR A DICTATOR:

The full implication of Miss Pratt's speech is that people do not know what is good for them. Only a benevolent dictator does. That brain-washing citizens, through a nation-wide curriculum, enforced by state schools, is the only way to generate virtue, discard vice, and purify people's souls, so they can become part of something ostensibly greater than themselves, the *mythos* of a perfect collective utopia.

(78) ANALYSIS OF WHY FOUGLER HATES WEBB:

Fougler hates Webb not only because Webb wants to kill the *very* people he depends on to live (i.e. individuals he needs to exist) but Fougler also hates Webb because he believes that literary creation (especially dramaturgy) is a waste of time. Accordingly, Webb claims he will eliminate *all* serious literature in his new Marxist world government, thus rendering Fougler's profession obsolete.

(79) ANALYSIS OF HOW FOUGLER WILL SURVIVE UNDER TOOHEY'S MARXIST DICTATORSHIP:

Evidently, Fougler is a third-rate drama critic who Toohey elevates to a literary prominence he does not deserve not because he is talented and merits it but because he is a *yes man* who will help Toohey destroy drama so he can take over the field. Sensing, then, that his role as a drama critic will cease to exist in Toohey's communist world government, Fougler tries to reinvent himself anew by recasting himself as a critic hostile to all theatre except worker's theater.

This is why Fougler says that "in the world of the future theater will not be necessary at all [since] the daily life of the common man is as much a work of art in itself as the best Shakespearian tragedy" (583). Here, Fougler tries to create a niche for himself in a future Marxist world government, since he wants to be relevant in a new world he thinks is coming. Thus, Fougler begins to create communist rhetoric that will not only enable him to survive under World Marxism but will also enable him to earn a living through some form of dramatic analysis. This is also why Fougler says that "...in the future there will be no need for the dramatist [since the] critic will simply observe the life of the masses and evaluate its artistic points for the public" (583). Here, Fougler yields to Toohey's attempt to replace good drama (plays that examine not things as they are but things as they ought to be) with bad drama (plays covering the ordinary, mundane, and trite) because he is not brave enough to go against the person who picks him out of obscurity and elevates him to a perch he does not deserve. Ironically, though Fougler begets his own destruction as a dramatist by undercutting literary values, he still goes along with Toohey's plan for world domination, since he would rather be an evil somebody than a good nobody. In essence, Fougler knows that he is a failed playwright and a terrible drama critic who would have remained an obscure nothing if it was not for Toohey raising him to an elevated literary station.

(80) ANALYSIS OF MITCHELL LAYTON'S CHARACTER ESPECIALLY IN COMPARISON TO HENRY CAMERON'S:

Evidently, Mitchell Layton is a disorderly, frenetic, offensive half-wit, who conveys his morose mood with a permanent scowl, frequently barking his displeasure at others, as demonstrated when he loses all self-control when he yells at the *Banner's* board. Despite Layton's apoplectic venting, however, the *Banner's* board, like most people, do not take his ideas seriously about anything, since he is a chronic complainer with no real substance. Thus, it is no wonder why people do not listen to, or generously receive, Mitchell Layton's bizarre ideas about anything, since his wealth does not automatically qualify his ideas to be adopted.

Make no mistake, Mitchell Layton's toxic personality is not to be confused with Henry Cameron's crotchety cantankerousness, since the two men are very different.

Though both men have troubled personalities Henry Cameron is a temperamental genius at heart with real substance—despite his outer layer of bitterness—while Mitchell Layton is just a blowhard clacking his uppers. For Henry Cameron is a superlative genius who creates the modern skyscraper, while Mitchell Layton is a silly ignoramus, who has never done anything worthwhile. Thus, while Cameron's bitterness is justified, since *most* of humanity does not recognize or appreciate his genius, Layton's crabbiness is totally uncalled for.

In sum, Henry Cameron is entitled to be angry, since anger, as Ayn Rand tells us, is a total emotional response to a real injustice, while petulant temper-tantrums a la Mitchell Layton, is totally unjustified, with no redeeming value whatsoever.

That said, chronic anger, in both of these individuals, whether justified—in Henry Cameron's case, or baseless, in Mitchell Layton's case—does not help either of these men in anyway. Yet the cognoscente are willing to listen to Henry Cameron, since deep-down, they respect him, despite what they say publicly, while people only tolerate Mitchell Layton, because he has deep pockets.

(81) ANALYSIS OF WHY RENEE PRATT MARRIES HOMER SLOTTERN AND THE ROLE HER SISTER PLAYS IN RAISING HER:

Renee Pratt-Slottern is a timid creature who is so thoroughly dominated by her sister that she marries Homer Slottern, essentially because her sister wants to connect her "old family name" to Homer's personal fortune (580). Bereft of a distinct individuality of her own – complete with her own motivations, interests, inclinations, and free will – Renee wonders how it would feel to actually want something instead of automatically yielding to the wishes of others.

She feels this way because Jessica Pratt limits her sister's free speech to certain topics, like rich men for example, while suppressing her opinions in other areas, like politics, for instance, thereby coopting her sister's personality to get what she wants.

Yes, Jessica Pratt thinks she loves her sister—and maybe she does, in her own way. Yet she does not let Renee find her own persona. Instead, she matches Renee to a wealthy man who can not only afford to lavish her with an exquisite house, elegant vehicles, and fine dresses but who can also vary her social entertainment by taking her to theatres, keeping her on his arm at social parties, and taking her on extravagant vacations. Renee, unfortunately, does not choose a lavish lifestyle for herself; nor does she choose her husband. Rather, she lives an accommodated life living as a kept-creature, unable to make serious decisions on her own.

Yet Renee's greatest downfall regards romance, since love, is "a response to a person's values" (AR). Yet Renee does not choose her husband according to her values. Thus, she feels empty inside.

In brief, since Jessica "dedicates her life to Renee's upbringing," she warps Renee's soul in her formative years, instead of uplifting her being like a good surrogate mother should (581).

(82) ANALYSIS OF RENEE'S INNOCENCE:

Renee, it seems, is an honest, innocent, harmless soul, who cannot fathom how a person, such as Ellsworth Toohey, who works for a company, such as *The Banner*, could serreptiously corrode that business while pretending to work for its' best interests. Indeed, her *naivete* is her most redeeming feature because while Renee is not clever and cunning like her plotting associates *most* readers appreciate her innocence (at least I do) since she embodies the ordinary virtues that regular decent folks have. In other words, Renee is cleaner than her immediate social circle, since she is a really honest person who does not understand the underhanded Machiavellian machinations employed by Toohey and others. This is to her credit. It is actually a positive. It is a good thing. A plus to her character, since she does not think like an immoral person.

Some people may say that Rene is too sheltered, not shrewd enough, not wise to the ways of the world. My stance, though, is that it is better to be innocent of venality even if it renders a person unperceptive, then to be jaded by human vice. In sum, since Renee's sister, Jessica, calls Renee "a child [who] shouldn't bother with dirty politics" Renee is kept ignorant in her adolescence and teenage years about the precise nature of her sister's "fraudulent intrigues, underhanded "scheme[s]," and incessant "plots," to marry her to Homer Slottern (585). Thus, Renee is kept pure, despite being mentally inert.

In essence, then, the lesson to be learned from Renee's characterization is that it is better to be an honest person with moral values even if you are not so smart then to be a *snollygoster* who lies often.

(83) ANALYSIS OF WHY WYNAND FEELS RESPONSIBLE FOR CREATING THE BEET LEAF THROWER:

Evidently, Wynand feels responsible for corrupting people like the rotten beet leaf thrower, since he regularly delivers vices to them over many years by writing morally reprehensible stories in *the Banner* on a quotidian basis, which his readers eagerly lap-up during their lives. Said differently, by repeatedly bombarding the rotten beet leaf thrower (and her ilk) with decadent stories about vice and human corruption, Wynand distorts her mishapen soul in the first place. To the extent that she acts outs. Thus, taking pity on her stunted being Wynand releases the rotten beet leaf thrower, since he recognizes that without his *Banner* she would have been a better person.

(84) ANALYSIS OF HOW TOOHEY NOT ONLY SEEKS TO CONTROL MR. TALBOT'S NEWSPAPER THE COURIER BUT ALSO HOW TIME IS RUNNING OUT FOR TOOHEY:

The radio remark "time marches on" suggests that though Toohey will try to take-over another newspaper by manipulating and controlling its owner—just like he did with Wynand's *Banner*—ultimately his time is running out (722). One day in the not too distant future Toohey will lack the mental and physical capacity to spin his power-grabbing schemes anymore, since he is aging, growing old, and thus on the decline, since time inevitably passes by.

In sum, readers sense that Toohey's defeat on the *Banner* is a blow from which he cannot easily recover (if at all) since his creeping *senescence* undermines his ability to serreptiously corrode another newspaper.

(85) ANALYSIS OF MRS. WILMOT'S FEELINGS OF ENTITLEMENT:

Mrs. Wilmot rankles at the idea that an architect—any architect but especially Howard Roark—could have the audacity to challenge her architectural judgment, since she is used to people automatically adhering to her opinions in courtesy deference. Because of her wealth. This is why Mrs. Wilmot bristles at the idea that an architect could have the gall to disobey her, since she feels she is an architectural expert worthy of respect, since she took a course on architecture at her local country club, which qualifies her as an architectural expert. Thus, she is shocked that Roark refuses to build according to her specifications, since she feels that her husband's vast wealth entitles her to bark authoritative commands at others, which must be obeyed without question, even if her demands contradicts Roark's better judgment. Indeed, since Mrs. Wilmot thinks she has an Elizabethan personality she expects all people to follow her dictates on command, since she feels that her judgment is absolute on all matters, including building.

(86) ANALYSIS OF THE INEFFECTIVENESS OF THE AQUITANIA BOARD:

It is not so important who Mr. Thompson, Mrs. Pritchett, and Mr. Macy are; nor what they say. What is important is that there is a lot of hearsay gossip about what should or should not be done about the Aquitania Hotel and why. Yet none of the Aquitania board members will say what they think should be done about Roark until they believe the other board members feel the same way, since they do not want to stand out in anyway because they do not want to be a human nail that gets hammered down. Rather, they want to match their views to the opinions of other board members, so they don't stick out in any way.

Sadly, the overall result of their equivocation is a hung board where all dodge responsibility and nothing gets done.

(87) ANALYSIS OF HOW AQUITANIA BOARD MEMBERS ARE ME-TOOER'S:

While this board member claims to make up his own mind independent of what other people think, ironically he does not found his opinions on objective facts or rational evidence. Rather, he is *also* a me-tooer who regurgitates what others think about Roark.

(88) ANALYSIS OF HOW THE AQUITANIA BUILDING & HOWARD ROARK'S CAREER ARE BOTH STILL-BORN PROJECTS:

The old watchman of the Aquitania Hotel subconsciously compares the corpse of the Aquitania building (i.e. its "rooms without ceilings, [spaces without] floors, and shivering planks that [hang] over the emptiness," to his stillborn son to express the idea that like his progeny miscarried Roark's brainchild also miscarried (346). Ayn Rand's use of symbols, here, replete with her description that "the open edges of the [Aquitania Hotel]—with girders that [stuck] out like bones through a broken skin"—links the idea of his son dying in birth to Roark's building dying in birth too.

(89) ANALYSIS OF HOW TOOHEY EXPLOITS HIS FATHER'S LACK OF BUSINESS ACUMEN:

Since his father, Horace Toohey is greatly saddened by his lack of business acumen, his son, Ellsworth Toohey, pounces on this hidden source of lament, twice, to rub salt in Mr. Toohey's wounds. Once in connection to his classmate's father owning a drygoods store. And again, when he tells his mother that Pat Noonan's father runs his "own ice-cream parlor" (303). Evidently, when Ellsworth Toohey does not get his way (i.e. when he does not get that new bike or that new suit) he pours scorn on his father. Outwardly, however, Ellsworth seems to behave like a considerate young man, since he rejects unnecessary material possessions in light of his family's modest budget. Yet, really, Toohey sneers at his father's sorest point to hurt him in the deepest way he can. Thus, Toohey's honey-tongued comments are actually mixed with scalding acid to mortify his interlocutors: In this case his father. In sum, even though Toohey seems innocent he actually masks his deep inner-evil by making hurtful comments: Castigations that *most* people are not astute enough to pick-up on.

(90) ANALYSIS OF HOW BOTTLE CAPS STOMPED INTO N.Y.C.'S STREETS SYMBOLIZE WYNAND'S FALL:

Just like bottle caps are stomped into the streets by the city's public Wynand is also discarded by the city's urban dwellers.

(91) ANALYSIS OF WYNAND'S PLEASURE PAIN REACTION TO ROARK:

This scene juxtaposes reverence for Roark, on the one hand, signaled by Wynand looking up to him, together with pain, on the other, signaled by Wynand pulling his throat muscles to look up. Since this scene comes at a time when Wynand talks to Dominique about whether Roark is a shrine or a hair shirt, it signals that Wynand's respect for Roark is alloyed with pain. He admires Roark, on the one hand, for his uncompromising genius. But he is also pained by him, on the other hand, since Roark reminds him of his failings as a man.

ARCHITECTURAL WORDS

Architrave: The lowermost part of a raised horizontal structure resting directly on top of a column in classical architecture.

Bas-Relief: A type of relief (sculpture) that has less depth to the faces and figures than they actually have, when measured proportionately (to scale). This technique retains the natural contours of the figures, and allows the work to be viewed from many angles without distortion of the figures themselves.

Buttress: A projecting structure of masonry or wood for supporting or giving stability to a wall or building (as to resist lateral pressure or strain acting at a particular point in one direction).

Capital: The top part, or head, of a pillar or column.

Cartouche: A scroll shaped architectural ornament sometimes used for inscriptions.

Colonnade: A series of columns placed at regular intervals.

Conduit: A natural or artificial channel through which water or other fluids passes or is conveyed: Aqueduct. Pipe.

Cornice: The typically molded and projecting horizontal member that crowns an architectural composition.

Corinthian Columns: Since Corinth is in Greece, Corinthian Column refers to the most ornate of the three classical orders of architecture, characterized by a slender fluted column of architecture, that has an ornate bell-shaped capitol decorated with acanthus leaves.

Dado: The section of a pedestal between the base and the crown.

Doric Portico: A porch or walkway with a roof supported by columns, often leading to the entrance of a building belonging to the oldest and simplest of the ancient Greek architectural orders.

Dormer: A window set vertically in a small gable projecting from a sloping roof.

Entablature: 1) The upper section of a classical order, resting on the capital and including the architrave, frieze, and cornice 2) A raised horizontal structure.

Eaves: The projecting overhang at the lower edge of a roof.

Façade: 1) The front of a building 2) The face of a building, especially a principal face.

Fenestration: The design and placement of windows in a building.

Five Orders: There are five major orders of architecture:

1) Doric (Greek)
2) Ionic (Greek)
3) Corinthian (Greek)
4) Tuscan (Roman)
5) Composite

The Doric order is the oldest and simplest of the ancient Greek architectural orders. The Ionic order is the second oldest order of classical Greek architecture that is lighter and more graceful than Doric. The Corinthian order belongs to the lightest and most ornate of the three Greek orders. The Tuscan is another classical order of architecture that is of Roman origin and is of plain style. The fifth order of architecture is a composite order that combines the volutes of the Ionic with the leaves of the Corinthian Order.

Fiat Pilasters: An upright architectural member of ancient Rome that is rectangular in plan and is structurally a pier but architecturally treated as a column, which may be load bearing or merely applied as surface decoration. Fiat means let it be done.

Florentine Balcony: A Renaissance balcony in Florence Italy that is an unroofed platform projecting from a wall of a building enclosed by a railing and resting on brackets or consoles.

Flying Buttress: A buttress slanting from a separate pier, typically forming an arch with the wall it supports.

Frieze: A sculptured or richly ornamented band on a building in classical architecture that is horizontal and rests on a column.

Gable: The vertical triangular portion of the end of a building from the level of the cornice or eaves to the ridge of the roof.

Garland of Gilded Fruit: A wreath cast in metal of various fruits.

Gambrel Roofs: A ridged roof with two slopes on each side, the lower slope having the steeper pitch.

Girder: A horizontal beam, as of steel or wood, used as a main support for a building or other structure.

Gothic: The word Gothic is derived from the **Goths** who were barbarians lacking in culture and refinement since they were members of an east Germanic people that in the early centuries of the Christian era overran the Roman Republic. **Gothic fiction** is characterized by the use of medieval settings, a murky atmosphere of horror and gloom, and macabre, mysterious, and violent incidents. Similarly, **Gothic Architecture** consists of stone structures, gargoyles, large expanses of stained glass, clustered columns, sharply pointed spires, intricate sculptures, ribbed vaults, and flying buttresses.

Ionic Snails: A sculpted plaster snail shell ornament belonging to second oldest order of ancient Greek architecture.

Ionic Columns: Ionic columns are high slender fluted columns.

Lintel: The horizontal beam that forms the upper member of a window or door frame and supports part of the structure above it.

Mezzanine: A partial story between the two main stories of a building. Usually, the mezzanine level is between the ground floor and the first floor.

Parapet: A low, protective wall or railing along the edge of a roof, balcony, or similar structure.

Pediment: The triangular space forming the gable of a pitched roof in classical architecture.

Pilaster: A pillar or column with a capital and base, set into a wall as an ornamental motif.

Pitched Roof: A pitched roof is a roof that slopes downwards, typically in two parts at an angle from a central ridge. The pitch of a roof is its vertical rise and is a measure of its steepness.

Stringcourse: A horizontal band or molding set in the face of a building as a design element.

Trellis: A frame supporting open latticework used for training vines and other growing plants.

Vaulted: An arched structure, usually of stone, brick, or concrete, forming a ceiling or a roof.

Volute: A spiral, scroll-like ornament such as that used on an Ionic capital.

Balustrade: A rail and row of posts that support it, as along the edge of a staircase or balcony.

AYN RAND'S (FICTION & NONFICTION)

AYN RAND'S FICTION

Title	Publisher	Division	Imprint	Location	1ˢᵗ Edition	Reprint
The Fountainhead	Penguin Putnam	Signet Classic	New American Library	New York City	1943	2016
Atlas Shrugged	Penguin Putnam	Signet Classic	New American Library	New York City	1957	1992
Anthem	Cayote Canyon Press	N / A	N / A	Claremont California	1938	1995
We the Living	Penguin Putnam	Signet Classic	New American Library	New York City	1936	1996
Ideal	Penguin Group	N / A	New American Library	New York City	1983	2015
Night of January 16 th Originally Published as: _Penthouse Legend_	Penguin Group	Plume	N / A	New York City	1933	1987
Think Twice _Ayn Rand Three Plays_	Penguin Group	Signet Classic	New American Library	New York City	1984	**2005**

AYN RAND'S NON-FICTION

Title	Publisher	Division	Imprint	Location	1ˢᵗ Edition	Reprint
Capitalism: _The Unknown Ideal_	Penguin Group	Signet	New American Library	New York City	1966	2000
The Virtue of Selfishness: A New Concept of Egoism	Penguin Group	Signet	New American Library	New York City	1964	2007
The Romantic Manifesto: A Philosophy of Literature	Penguin Putnam	Signet	New American Library	New York City	1969	1975
Philosophy: _Who Needs It_	Penguin Group	Signet	New American Library	New York City	1982	2000
Ayn Rand Answers: The Best of Her Q & A	Penguin Group	N / A	New American Library	New York City	2005	2005
Objectively Speaking: Ayn Rand Interviewed	Rowman & Littlefield Publishers	Lexington Books	N / A	Lanham MD	2009	2009
Introduction to Objectivist Epistemology	Penguin Group	Dutton Signet	Meridian Books	New York City	1979	1990
The Art of Fiction: A Guide For Writers & Readers	Penguin Group	Plume	N / A	New York City	2000	2000
The Art of Nonfiction: A Guide For Writers & Readers	Penguin Books	Plume	N / A	New York City	2001	2001

The Return of the Primitive: The Anti-Industrial Revolution	Penguin Group	Dutton NAL	Meridian Books	New York City	1999	1999
The Ayn Rand Column: Written for the Los Angeles Times	The Ayn Rand Institute Press	N / A	N / A	Irvine California	1991	1998
For the New Intellectual	Penguin Group	Signet	New American Library	New York City	1963	2000
Journals of Ayn Rand	Penguin Group	Plume	N / A	New York City	1997	1997
Letters of Ayn Rand	Penguin Group	Plume	N / A	New York City	1995	1995

AYN RAND'S FICTION (CHRONOLOGY):

+ Ideal;
+ Think Twice;
+ Night of January 16 th (1933);
+ We the Living (1936);
+ Anthem (1938);
+ The Fountainhead (1943);
+ Atlas Shrugged (1957);

AYN RAND'S NON-FICTION (CHRONOLOGY):

+ For the New Intellectual (1963);
+ The Virtue of Selfishness (1964);
+ Capitalism: The Unknown Ideal (1966);
+ The Romantic Manifesto (1969);

+ Introduction to Objectivist Epistemology (1979);
+ Philosophy Who Needs It (1982);
+ The Ayn Rand Column (1991);
+ The Return of the Primitive (1999);
+ The Art of Fiction (2000);
+ The Art of Nonfiction (2001);
+ Ayn Rand Answers (2005);
+ Objectively Speaking: Ayn Rand Interviewed (2009);
+ Letters of Ayn Rand (1995);
+ Journals of Ayn Rand (1997);

OBJECTIVIST INTELLECTUALS SPREAD SHEET

Name	Affiliation	Contact	Work(s)	Date	Publisher
Shoshana Milgram-Knapp	Associate Professor of English at Virginia Tech	E-Mail: dashiell@vt.edu T: (540) 231-8462 Address: 227 Shanks Hall 181 Turner St. NW Blacksburg, VA 24061	Essays on Ayn Rand's The Fountainhead The Fountainhead from Notebook to Novel: The Composition of AR's First Ideal Man Three Inspirations for the Ideal Man: Cyrus Paltons; Enjolaras; and Cyrano de Bergerac	2007	Lexington Books

Michael S. Berliner	Taught Philosophy of Education and Philosophy at California State University (Northridge) * Former Executive Director of the Ayn Rand Institute (15 Years)	N / A Wrote Letters of Ayn Rand Writes for *Capitalism* Magazine	Essays on Ayn Rand's The Fountainhead *Howard Roark and Frank Lloyd Wright* *The Fountainhead Reviews*	2007	Lexington Books
Richard E. Ralston	Former Managing Director of ARI Former Circulation Director and Publishing Director Christian Science Monitor Presently Executive Director of Americans for Free Choice in Medicine Publishing Manager ARI	E-Mail: rralston@ aynrand.org T: (949) 222-6550 X 237	Essays on Ayn Rand's The Fountainhead *Publishing the Fountainhead*	2007	Lexington Books

Jeff Briting	Archivist AR Archives	E-Mail: jbritting@ aynrand.org	Essays on Ayn Rand's The Fountainhead *Adapting the Fountainhead to Film*	2007	Lexington Books
Tore Boeckman	Editor of AR's Art of Fiction Writer in Buffalo, NY	E-Mail: Loevborg62@ roadrunner.com Facebook Instant Messenger: @toreboeckmann	Essays on Ayn Rand's The Fountainhead *The Fountainhead as a Romantic Novel* *What Might Be Ought to Be: Aristotle's Poetics and The Fountainhead*	2007	Lexington Books

Andrew Bernstein	PhD. Philosophy C.U.N.Y.	Website:	CliffNotes on Rand's The Fountainhead	2000 2007 2009 2008	Houghton Mifflin Harcourt
		https://www. andrewbernstein. net/			
	Taught at Pace U & S.U.N.Y. Purchase		Essays on Ayn Rand's The Fountainhead	2019 (Spr)	Lexington Books
		E-Mail:	Understanding the "Rape"		
	Wrote cliff notes on all of AR's fiction	andyswoop@ gmail.com	Scene in The Fountainhead		For Beginners (Documentary
		Mail:	Ayn Rand For		Comic Book)
		The Ayn Rand Institute 4640 Admiralty Way Suite 406 Mariana del Rey, CA 90292	Beginners		
			Objectivism in One Lesson: An Introduction to the Philosophy of Ayn Rand		Hamilton Books
			Heroes of Great Literature		The Objectivist Standard (Vol. 14, No. 1)

Robert Mayhew	Prof. Philo. Seton Hall	E-Mails: experts@ aynrand.org robert.mayhew@ shu.edu Mail: Seton Hall University Department of Philosophy South Orange, NJ 07079 Fahy Hall Room 311 T: (973) 761-9000 X 5188	Essays on Ayn Rand's The Fountainhead Humor in The Fountainhead	2007	Lexington Books
John B. Bayer	M.A. Philosophy U Illinois Urbana-Champaign. ABD PhD U Illinois Urbana-Champaign. Teacher Philo U Illinois. Specialist in Epistemology	Lives in Burbank California	Essays on Ayn Rand's The Fountainhead The Fountainhead and the Spirit of Youth	2007	Lexington Books

Onkar Ghate	PhD. Philosophy University of Calgary. Senior Fellow ARI. Teacher of Philosophy at Ayn Rand Institute (Objectivist Academic Center). Chief Philosophy Officer at the Ayn Rand Institute	E-Mail: oghate@ aynrand.org	Essays on Ayn Rand's The Fountainhead *The Basic Motivation of the Creators and the Masses in The Fountainhead*	2007	Lexington Books
Debi Ghate	Vice President of Academic Programs at the Ayn Rand Institute Senior Director of the Anthem Foundation For Objectivist Scholarship Writer For Capitalism Magazine	Mail: Ayn Rand Institute 2121 Alton Parkway, Suite 250 Irvine, CA 92606	Editor of Why Businessmen Need Philosophy: *The Capitalists Guide to the Ideas Behind Ayn Rand's Atlas Shrugged*	2011	New American Library

Tara Smith	Prf. Philo. UT Austin Concentrates on Law but Writes on Other Topics	E-Mail: tara@austin. utexas.edu Campus Mail Code: C3500 The College of Liberal Arts The University of Texas at Austin 116 Inner Campus Dr. Mail Stop G6000 Austin, TX 78712	Essays on Ayn Rand's The Fountainhead Unborrowed Vision: Independence and Egoism in The Fountainhead	2007	Lexington Books
Dina Schein	Visiting Assistant Professor at Auburn University	R.I.P. (1969-2016) Cancer	Essays on Ayn Rand's The Fountainhead Roark's Integrity	2007	Lexington Books
Amy Peikoff	Assistant Prof. Philo US Air Force Academy. Associate Professor of Law. Research Fellow for the Study of Objectivism.	E-Mail: apeikoff@swlaw. edu T: (213) 738-6803 Office: BW345	Essays on Ayn Rand's The Fountainhead A Moral Dynamiting	2007	Lexington Books

Leonard Peikoff	A.R.'s Intellectual and Legal Heir	Website: www.peikoff.com	Essays on Ayn Rand's The Fountainhead An Interview With Leonard Peikoff (Epilogue)	2007	Lexington Books
Harry Binswanger	Ayn Rand Institute (Board of Directors) Taught Philosophy at Hunter College, The New School for Social Research, and UT Austin	E-Mail: scholars@aynrand.org	How We Know: Epistemology on an Objective Foundation	2015	CreateSpace Independent Publishing Program
Gregory Salmieri	Rutgers University / Boston University / University of North Carolina (Chapel Hill) / Pittsburg University	E-Mail: scholars@aynrand.org gregory.salmieri@rutgers.edu	Foundations of a Free Society: Reflections on Ayn Rand's Political Philosophy	2019	University of Pittsburgh Press
John Lewis	Objectivist Scholar Political Scientist Historian	R.I.P. January 3rd 2012	Early Greek Lawgivers	2007	Bristol Classical Press

John Ridpath	Professor of Economics and Intellectual History York University (Retired)		Ayn Rand vs. Karl Marx (MP3 Download)		
Yaron Brook	Chairman of ARI Former Executive Director of ARI (2000-2017)	experts@ aynrand.org Twitter: @ yaronbrook https://ari. aynrand. org/experts/ yaron-brook	Free Market Revolution: How Ayn Rand's Can End Big Government	2013	St. Martin's Griffin
Don Watkins	ARI Fellow (2006-2017)	E-Mail: dwatkins@ aynrand.org	Equal is Unfair: America's Misguided Fight Against Income Inequality	2016	St. Martin's Press
Alex Epstein	President and Founder of Center for Industrial Progress	Website: https://industrial progress.com/ Mail: Center for Industrial Progress 302 Washington St. #150-9385 San Diego, CA 92103	The Moral Case For Fossil Fuels	2014	Portfolio Hardcover

Peter Schwartz	Distinguished Fellow Ayn Rand Institute	Website: www. peterschwartz. com ARI Profile: https://ari. aynrand. org/experts/ peter-schwartz	In Defense of Selfishness: *Why The Code of Self-Sacrifice is Unjust and Destructive*	2015	Palgrave Macmillan
Elan Journo	Director and Senior Fellow Ayn Rand Institute	ARI Profile: https://ari. aynrand. org/experts/ elan-journo	What Justice Demands: *America and the Israeli-Palestinian Conflict*	2018	Post Hill Press
Lisa Van Damme	Founder of VanDamme Academy (Private Elementary & Junior High School)	VanDamme Academy Profile: https://www. vandamme academy.com/ lisa-vandamme	Teaching Values in the Classroom (Article for the Objectivist Standard)	2006	N / A
Jason Rheins	Assistant Professor of Philosophy Loyola University Chicago	Academia.edu Resume: https://luc. academia.edu/ JasonRheins/ CurriculumVitae Academia.edu Profile: https://luc. academia.edu/ JasonRheins	The Sublime Art: *An Introduction to the Elements of Poetry*	2006	Objectivist Summer Conference (San Diego)

Steve Simpson	Director of Legal Studies at ARI (2013-2018)	ARI Profile: https://ari.aynrand.org/experts/steve-simpson	An Orientation to Objectivism – Why Laissez-Faire	2016	Objectivist Summer Conference (2016)
Edwin A. Locke	Psychologist and Pioneer of Goal Setting Theory Retired Dean's Professor of Motivation & Leadership University of Maryland	ARI Campus Profile: https://campus.aynrand.org/people/edwin-locke	Study Methods & Motivations: A Practical Guide to Effective Study	1998	Second Renaissance
Ryan Krause	Ryan Krause, assistant professor of Strategy at the Neeley School of Business, Texas Christian University	TCU Profile: http://neeley.tcu.edu/AboutNeeley/Faculty_and_Staff/Krause,_Ryan.aspx	In Defense of Monopolies: How Antitrust Criminalizes Business Strategy	2015	Objectivist Summer Conference (Charlotte, NC)
Thomas Bowden	Former Analyst & Outreach Liaison at the Ayn Rand Institute		The Enemies of Christopher Columbus	2007	The Paper Tiger
Eric Daniels	Clemson University's Institute for the Study of Capitalism Writes for Capitalism Magazine	Capitalism Magazine Blog RSS Livestream: https://www.capitalismmagazine.com/author/EricDaniels/	Freedom of Speech in American History (MP3 Download)	2008	Objectivist Summer Conference (Newport Beach CA)

John Allison	Former CEO of CATO Institute Former CEO of BB & T Bank	Wikipedia Profile: https://en.wikipedia.org/wiki/John A. Allison IV	The Financial Crisis and the Free Market Cure	2012	McGraw-Hill Education
	Executive-in-Residence Wake Forest School of Business	Wake Forest University Profile: http://capitalism.wfu.edu/authors/john-a-allison-iv/			
Amanda Maxham	Science Writer (High Energy Astrophysics)	The Heartland Institute Profile: https://www.heartland.org/about-us/who-we-are/amanda-maxham	The Incredible Edible Genetically Modified Organism	2014	Objectivist Summer Conference (Las Vegas)
Gary Hull	Senior Writer for ARI (1997-2002) Professor at Duke University Director of the Program on Values and Ethics in the Marketplace	N / A	The Abolition of Anti-Trust (Editor)	2005	Transaction Publishers

| Adam Mossoff | Law Professor at George Mason

Founder and Executive Director of the Center for the Protection of Intellectual Property | George Mason University Profile:

https://www.law.gmu.edu/faculty/directory/fulltime/mossoff_adam | Intellectual Property and Property Rights | 2013 | Edward Elgar Publishing |
|---|---|---|---|---|---|
| Rituparna Basu | Analyst at the Ayn Rand Institute

Penn. State Bachelors of Science Former President Penn State Objectivists | N / A | Understanding the Arguments for Universal Health Care | 2015 | Objectivist Summer Conference (Charlotte, NC) |
| Carl Svanberg | Research Associate Ayn Rand Institute (2013-2018)

Objectivist Academic Center Graduate | Twitter:

@ CarlSvandeburg | What About Sweden | 2013 | Objectivist Summer Conference (Chicago) |

| John L. Dennis | Professor Department of Psychology University of Alberta

PhD University of Texas at Austin | Academia.edu Profile:

https://unipg. academia.edu/ JohnDennis

Academia.edu Resume:

https://unipg. academia.edu/ JohnDennis/ CurriculumVitae | Changing Habits: *Why It's Hard, How to Do It* | 2012 | Objectivist Summer Conference (San Diego) |
|---|---|---|---|---|---|
| Ray Girn | Founder of Higher Ground Education (Promotes Montessori Education)

LePort Schools K-8 Lab School (Lead a Team of Educators in Architecting LePort's Upper School and Curriculum Program) | Higher Ground Education Profile:

https://www. tohigherground. com/about/ray-girn | The Self-Made Child: *Maria Montessori's Philosophy of Education* | 2014 | Objectivist Summer Conference (Las Vegas) |

John David Lewis	Visiting Associate Professor in Philosophy, Politics, & Economics at Duke University Adjunct Associate Professor of Business at University of North Carolina at Chapel Hill	R.I.P. (1955-2012) Website: https://www. johndavidlewis. com/	Early Greek Lawgivers	2007	Bristol Classical Press
Amesh Adalja	Senior Scholar John's Hopkin's University Center for Health Security	John's Hopkin's Profile: http://www. center forhealthsecurity. org/our-staff/ profiles/adalja/	Vaccination: An Essentialized of an Essential Technology	2016	Objectivist Summer Conference (Seattle)
Ben Bayer	Instructor and Fellow at the Ayn Rand Institute	ARI Profile: https://ari. aynrand. org/experts/ ben-bayer	A Brief History of the Concept of Free Will	2013	Objectivist Summer Conference (Chicago)
Talbot Manvel	Retired Navy Captain Graduate of Naval Academy, St. John's College, and the Ayn Rand Institute	E-Mail: talmanvel@ icloud.com	Aircraft Carrier: Defending America on the Seas and in the Air (MP3 Download)	N/A	N / A

C. Bradley Thompson	BB&T Research Professor at Clemson University and the Executive Director of the Clemson Institute for the Study of Capitalism	Profile CATO Unbound (Journal): https://www. cato-unbound. org/contributors/ c-bradley-thompson	American Slavery / American Freedom (MP3 Download)	2007	Objectivist Summer Conference (Telluride, CO)
Martin Johansen	Computer Scientist and Developer at Inductive AS From Oslo Norway	Linked-In Profile: https:// no.linkedin. com/in/ martinfjohansen	Charles Babbage: *Induction in Computer Science* (MP3 Download)	2013	Chicago Illinois
Allan Gotthelf	American Philosopher (Scholar of Aristotle and Ayn Rand)	R.I.P. (1942-2013) Wikipedia Profile: https:// en.wikipedia. org/wiki/Allan Gotthelf	Aristotle as Scientist: *A Proper Verdict* *(MP3 Download)*	N /A	N / A
Andrew Lewis	Teacher at VanDamme Academy B.A. & M.A. degrees University of Melbourne	VanDamme Academy Profile: https://www. vandamme academy.com/ andrew-lewis	The Renaissance	2008	Objectivist Summer Conference 2008 (Newport Beach CA)

David Harriman	Objectivist Historian & Scientist Editor of Journals of Ayn Rand	N / A	The Journals of Ayn Rand	1997	Dutton
Barry Wood	Humanities Department Dixie State University	Academia.edu Profile: https://dixie. academia.edu/ BarryWood Academia.edu Resume: https://dixie. academia.edu/ BarryWood/ CurriculumVitae	The Battle Over Reason in the Islamic World (and How it Was Lost) (MP3 Download)	2012	Objectivist Summer Conference (San Diego)
Pat Corvini	Objectivist Intellectual	N / A	Achilles, the Tortoise, and the Objectivity of Mathematics	2005	Objectivist Summer Conference (San Diego, CA)

Stephen Plafker	Retired Los Angeles County Deputy District Attorney Founder of The Association for Objective Law Taught Math at Tulane University Writer For Capitalism Magazine	Objectivist Conference Profile: https://www.objectivistconferences.info/speakers/stephen-plafker	Structure of the American Constitution (MP3 Download)	2006	Objectivist Summer Conference (Boston, MA)
Wilhelm Windelband	German Philosopher **(On The Ayn Rand Institute E-Store)**	Wikipedia Profile: https://en.wikipedia.org/wiki/Wilhelm_Windelband	A History of Philosophy: *With Especial Reference to the Formation and Development of its Problems and Conceptions* (Hardcover)	?	?
Jean Moroney	President of Thinking Directions	Thinking Directions Profile: https://www.thinkingdirections.com/about.htm	Aligning Your Subconscious Values With Your Conscious Convictions & Fueling Achievement with Objectivist Values	2015	Objectivist Summer Conference (Charlotte, NC)

Gena Gorlin	Bachelor of Science Tufts University	Psychology Today Listing: https://www.psychologytoday.com/us/therapists/gena-i-gorlin-new-york-ny/413351	Taking Responsibility for Your Happiness: *Insights From Contemporary Psychology* (MP 3 Download)	2016	Ayn Rand Student Conference 2016 (Atlanta)
Aaron Smith	Instructor & Fellow Ayn Rand Institute	Ayn Rand Experts Profile: https://ari.aynrand.org/experts/aaron-smith	Benevolence, Goodwill and the Rationally Selfish Life (MP3 Download)	2015	Objectivist Summer Conference (Charlotte, NC)
H.W.B. Joseph	British Philosopher	Wikipedia Profile: https://en.wikipedia.org/wiki/H._W._B._Joseph	An Introduction to Logic (Hardcover)	2000	Paper Tiger
Keith Lockitch	Vice President of Content & Senior Fellow at the Ayn Rand Institute	Ayn Rand Institute Profile: https://ari.aynrand.org/experts/keith-lockitch	Charles Darwin: More Than "Just a Theorist" (MP3 Download)	2007	Objectivist Summer Conference (Telluride, CO)
Ellen Kenner	Clinical Psychologist	Website: http://www.drkenner.com/	Bringing Out the Hero in Yourself (MP3 Download)	2004	Objectivist Summer Conference (Wintergreen VA)
Robert Knapp	Ph.D. Math Princeton University	Link to His Book: https://mathematicsisabouttheworld.com/	The Measure of All Things (MP3 Download)	2011	Objectivist Summer Conference (Fort Lauderdale, FL)

OBJECTIVIST INTELLECTUALS

* Some of the information in this table—like current affiliation and contact data—may no longer be accurate, since it was primarily assembled in 2017, mainly from the internet. Therefore, please verify before using.

* Please contact these scholars *only* if you *really need* to—if you have something important to discuss—since they are busy. As you know, you could always use this table to *just* support your research or to *just* understand what Objectivist Intellectuals think about Ayn Rand and her books.

Objectivist sources I will surely consult and probably use in my forthcoming *Fountainhead Analyzed* book are:

+ Bernstein's *Fountainhead Cliff Notes* (2000);
+ Bernstein's *AR for Beginners* (2009);
+ Bernstein's *Objectivism in One Lesson: An Introduction to the Philosophy of Ayn Rand* (2008);
+ Bernstein's *Understanding the Rape Scene in The Fountainhead* (2007);
+ Bernstein's *Heroes of Great Literature* (2009);
+ Milgram's *The Fountainhead from Notebook to Novel* (2007);
+ Berliner's *Howard Roark and Frank Lloyd Wright* (2007);
+ Berliner's *The Fountainhead Reviews* (2007);
+ Ralston's *Publishing The Fountainhead* (2007);
+ Britting's *Adapting The Fountainhead to Film* (2007);
+ Boeckmann's *The Fountainhead as a Romantic Novel* (2007);
+ Boeckmann's *What Might Be and Ought to Be: Aristotle's Poetics and The Fountainhead* (2007);
+ Mayhew's *Humor in The Fountainhead* (2007);
+ Bayer's *The Fountainhead and the Spirit of Youth* (2007);

- Ghate's *The Basic Motivation of the Creators and the Masses in The Fountainhead* (2007);
- Smith's *Unborrowed Vision: Independence and Egoism in The Fountainhead* (2007);
- Schien's *Roark's Integrity* (2007);
- Amy Peikoff's *A Moral Dynamiting*, and (2007);
- Leonard Peikoff's *Interview About The Fountainhead* (2007)

OUTRODUCTION: *EXPLANATION OF MY OBJECTIVIST INTELLECTUALS TABLE / DISCLAIMER FOR THIS REFERENCE GUIDE / EXPLANATION OF MY CHANGE IN PHILOSOPHY / APOLOGY FOR MY FORMER BOOKS / EXPLANATION OF MY JOB*

Since my goal is to accurately analyze Ayn Rand's books according to Objectivism—to enhance the clear reception of AR's ideas—I only reference Objectivist Intellectuals here.

To explain, I only *adduce* Objectivists intellectuals in the below table because even though there are non-objectivist-intellectuals who genuinely like Ayn Rand, honestly understand her ideas, and offer fairly accurate analysis, there are also *many* scholars who either misunderstand her ideas, or oppose her ideology, or distort her philosophy for their own ends. Thus, to avoid citing the scholarship of people who either misinterpret, or counter, or warp AR's ideas, I only list the works of proven Objectivist Intellectuals here. In order to guide all people, but especially youths, towards an Aristotelian-Objectivist philosophy.

Further, since my *Fountainhead Reference Guide* is *neither endorsed* by the Ayn Rand Institute *nor sanctioned* by any Objectivist Intellectual *some* of my ideas *may* not align with Objectivism. Ergo, before accepting my reasoning please read relevant materials from Ayn Rand herself, and Objectivist Intellectuals, as well, to verify if my ideas are correct, or not. If, after this process of study, you judge, from an educated perspective, that my ideas either match, or do not match, those of Ayn Rand, then please integrate, or disintegrate, my thoughts from your mind accordingly, since I *only* want you to synthesize Objectivist ideas. I do not want to mislead you. For even though I tried my level-best to accurately interpret *The Fountainhead*—according to my understanding and ability—possibly

I misunderstood a point or two. If this is so please forgive me. It is not intentional. It is only an error of understanding and knowledge. For this *Reference Guide* is simply an *attempt* to understand *The Fountainhead* better, so I can write an accurate essay book based on it.

Finally, this reference guide is not a traditional study guide. (As helpful as that is). Rather, it is my own inductive process of first "rolling around [the *Fountainhead's*] concretes like a cat in catnip" (AR). Then extrapolating general themes from *The Fountainhead's* facts. Accordingly, this *Reference Guide* does not summarize the book, analyze a few main characters, or explicate sundry themes, as many study guides do. Rather, this *Reference Guide* is simply pre-writing for my forthcoming essay book, since writing and understanding—like Mr. Peter Swartz said—are two separate processes.

In truth, after studying Objectivism for a decade: then applying objective principles to different books, I have learned that it is *impossible* to synergize AR's ideas with non-Aristotelian thought systems, because other ideologies are not compatible (or consistent) with Objectivism.

Further, my former books *were* less than good given the form of the book I analyzed coupled with my own ignorance. For this I apologize. I was just trying to write a good book. Writing a semi-bad book was not my intention. For I am an honest person who *just* needs to understand Objectivism better, not someone who is trying to subvert the philosophy.

Honestly, my philosophy has evolved from a mixed thought system that combines many different sets-of-ideas to a uni-polar objectivist philosophy only. In truth it took me 10 years to accept *most* of Ayn Rand's ideas. Not only since I read, and reread, her fiction and non-fiction, repeatedly—after which I came to agree with much of her reasoning—but also because I selectively absorbed the ideas of Objectivist Intellectuals during this time. Over the last decade, I was *just* trying to go from ignorance to knowledge from darkness to light from unawareness to astuteness. For this reason I studied a lot of ideas but especially Objectivism. Now, after a fairly long value quest I accept *most* of AR's ideas.

In this quest for knowledge I made some opponents – including Objectivists – who *may* have thought I was either ignorantly confused, or trying to corrupt objectivism—knowingly or unknowingly, consciously or subconsciously. This view is completely plausible and *perhaps partially accurate* but only from the stance that I was trying to help the movement but I *may have* harmed the movement, at times. For I did not know what I was doing [4]. And, as Ayn Rand suggested, not knowing what you are doing is very dangerous, since entering a battle semi-prepared is more harmful than not entering a battle at all. But I have learned from my mistake. So now I am methodically preparing to enter the intellectual war-of-ideas between Objectivism and all other non-Aristotelian thought systems. Accordingly, I will fight for Ayn Rand's ideas and hopefully help Objectivism win one day.

That said, in terms of what others *may* have done, I am completely *innocent* of any wrongdoing there. For I have nothing to do with anything that *might* have happened or that *might* still be happening. In fact, I don't even know about it. I just write my ideas and whatever happens happens. Yet I comprehend the Objectivist siege mentality completely, since many dishonest others try to warp Objectivism. Thus, *some* Objectivists – perhaps many – do not trust or like me, since they *probably* harbor suspicions that I am trying to undercut AR's ideas. This is not true. I am simply trying to understand her philosophy first, so I can write about it accurately later. While I hope you can believe me, I understand if you do not. Ultimately, it is up to you to judge. But I have told you the truth. That is all I can do. Now my conscience is clear.

Anyway, now that my philosophy has changed, I will signal this shift by disassociating this book from my former books by changing the title of this reference guide from *The Fountainhead Explained Reference Guide* to *The Fountainhead Reference Guide: A to Z*. Admittedly, this new name is not unique. But it is all I can think of. If anyone has a better title please suggest it.

Anyway, eventually, I will *take-down* my old website, since my ideology has now changed from the poly-logics of my previous essay

---

[4] Maybe, somehow, I am indirectly to blame for what might still be going on. But am I going to pay for the rest of my life for something that happened a long time ago?

collection to just an Objectivist stance [5]. Ergo, now I will focus all of my intellectual energies on analyzing only Ayn Rand's objectivist philosophy as shown in her fiction. To this end I will write four reference guides and four essay books—for a total of 8 books—on AR's *The Fountainhead*, *Atlas Shrugged*, *The Anthem*, and *We the Living*. This process will not only enable me to write about her books accurately this process will enable me to fully incorporate AR's values in my being.

Simultaneously, I will create a personal author website to promote AR's objectivist philosophy. Maybe one day, *perhaps* several years from now, Objectivist's will learn to accept and trust me. The sooner the better. But if they do not, it is fine. For all I need to understand Objectivism is Ayn Rand's books, supplemented by the writings of Objectivist Intellectuals. Possibly you guys-and-gals will eventually trust me enough to be friends with me. I guess this really depends on what I do and if I can be fully consistent. Because as some of you *may* know, I do backslide for several weeks a year for personal problems of my own, even though I work smart-and-hard, in my own way, for most of the year. But flashes of brilliance are not enough. One must maintain top-level performance all of the time. Consistently and indefatigably. I realize this. And strive for perfection. But sometimes I do falter. It is just a weakness in me. But when I weaken I do not bother anybody. I just keep to myself. And I am always fine in the end, especially after I recover. In the future, I will *try* to always be well—for 12 months of the year—since I believe I can *always* focus and should *always* focus, especially if I have help.

---

[5] Though, I know I should remove my website immediately, I find it difficult to erase a project I have worked on for ten years, since it inspires me with accomplishment and pride. Eventually, though, I will find the strength to remove it. But not right now. I am sorry for this moral failing. Yet rest assured as soon as I am able I will erase my former website and set-up a completely separate Ayn Rand website. Not only to promote her ideas but also to promote my ideas on her ideas.

Now, I would like to talk about my career. My career, despite popular belief, and a lot of criticism, is a literary map maker [6]. Though this career does not earn me much money, causes others to resent and mock me, and is a hard thankless life, I still do it, and can do nothing else, because that is who I am. It is my meaning, my purpose, and why I am alive. It is fun and brings me joy. And despite *status quo* thinkers who try to persuade me to work a job that neither connects to my identity nor uses my abilities my inner conscience tells me to keep writing. So that is what I am going to do despite any amount of pressure. For I have coped with systematic criticism – persecution even – for 12 years. I can cope with it *forever* if need be. But I hope pressurizing me is no longer needed (in fact it never was) because I do not want to be pressured. Further, some people do not want to pressure me either. If the powers that be could simply accept that I am working when I am writing then maybe they could just leave me alone? Anyway, some people are really tired of me anyway. I think they would feel relief if they could just forget about me. For I am sure they have much better things to do anyway with their time. For I am irrelevant to them [7]. That said, if it is between coping with pressure or sacrificing my values than pressure it is. For I will just ignore it – just like Roark ignores Toohey – so I can disinvolve myself from people's schemes and focus on my purpose instead.

Anyway as you probably realize, once an individual finds their life's purpose it is foolish to switch to anything else. Did Roark switch from architecture to something else? No. Did Steven Mallory switch from being a sculptor to something else? No. Did Mike Donnigan switch

---

[6] Please be glad that I am now *fully* on your side. For I think I understand objectivism fairly accurately, can write about it well—when I put my mind to it—and am an honest and moral person: at least on paper. And while I am not the most intelligent person in the world I think I am smarter than the average bear, at least when it comes to creating sets-of-ideas. But, admittedly, in other ways, I am average (at best) perhaps sub-average (at worst).

[7] I want precisely what some other people want for me and themselves. For me to get out of the mess I am in. We just disagree on the method of my exit. I want to get out by writing. They want me to get out by working some sort of meaningless job that is a waste of me. Well I will not. For I am already working.

from being a construction worker to something else? No. That is why I continue to write. This time about *Objectivism.*

And the only organization I will work for is an *Objectivist* one. I tried to work at ARI before but was outcompeted. But now I feel I qualify to be paid by Objectivists to write reference guides and essay books on Ayn Rand's fiction, since *I think* I understand the philosophy fairly well and write about it pretty accurately. Of course, I would revise my books per the editorials of objectivist intellectuals. So my ideas 100 % match Ayn Rand's objectivist philosophy. Therefore, I ask "might the appropriate Objectivist consider making me a freelance objectivist affiliate" [8]? Probably not. I had to ask though.

Regardless, I am going to write 8 books on all of AR's books. (Sorry, but that is final). For I have a *keen* ability to inspire the general culture with a value oriented moral direction; because when I write I do not warp my analysis for any authority figure, whoever they are or whatever they *might* either really know – or think they know but do not. That is *probably* why I do not like working for any boss whomsoever. And that is also why a lot of people hate me too. Either that, or they do not understand me. Or they fault me for not earning a steady paycheck. I do not care, for I will write books about AR's books regardless. That's all.

Anyway, writing is my highest purpose: a *reason d'etre* I will not change for anyone; nor for any reason; whatsoever. Because **making literary maps is my job.** One I take very seriously. Further, to create the literary maps I need to create, I feel I should be unaffiliated with any organization whatsoever, since I do not want anyone warping my ideas. Because I value the integrity of my thoughts as well as my freedom. That said, I do admire certain people, and will take orders from them, just like

---

[8] If objectivists do not want to engage with me for whatever reason, so be it. It is up to you. For if I was in your position I *likely* would not want to link with me either because of what *may* come with me as you *may* already be finding out. Ergo, if you feel I cannot help you, or that you do not need my help, or that you cannot jeopardize objectivism because of one inconsistent individual, I respect your decision. It's fine. You are free to do what you want. But I am also free to do what I want, too. As long as I do not violate anyone's rights or initiate force. So I am going to write my AR books. That is all.

Steven Mallory obeys Howard Roark, since Roark lets Mallory create statues his own way.

Lastly, I do not care about money or power for I will not betray who I am simply for a paycheck. Nor will I waste my time leading a pointless life doing something else that is a waste of me. Also I will not corrupt myself or my ideas for anyone or anything "for what gaineth a man if he sells his soul to get it."

April 26, 2019

Printed in the United States
By Bookmasters